Landmarks of world literature

Augustine

THE CONFESSIONS

Landmarks of world literature
General Editor: J. P. Stern

AUGUSTINE
The Confessions

GILLIAN CLARK
Lecturer in Classics, University of Liverpool

CAMBRIDGE
UNIVERSITY PRESS

Published by the Press Syndicate of the University of Cambridge
The Pitt Building, Trumpington Street, Cambridge CB2 1RP
40 West 20th Street, New York NY 10011-4211, USA
10 Stamford Road, Oakleigh, Victoria 3166, Australia

First published 1993

Printed in Great Britain at the University Press, Cambridge

A catalogue record for this book is available from the British Library

Library of Congress cataloguing in publication data
Clark, Gillian.
Augustine, the Confessions / Gillian Clark.
    p.   cm. – (Landmarks of world literature)
Includes bibliographical references.
ISBN 0-521-40104-6. – ISBN 0-521-40942-X (pbk.)
1. Augustine, Saint, Bishop of Hippo. Confessions.   I. Title.
II. Title: Confessions.   III. Series.
BR65.A62C53   1993
242 – dc20   92-41452   CIP

ISBN 0 521 40104 6 hardback
ISBN 0 521 40942 X paperback

27035638

Contents

vi   Contents

Preface

The *Confessions* is the most read and discussed of all Augustine's many books, and there is an overwhelming bibliography on every one of them. What I have chiefly tried to do, in this short introduction, is to set the *Confessions* in the context of 'late antiquity'. In the fourth and fifth centuries, the values of an inherited literary and philosophical culture were being challenged and a long-lasting political system was under threat. Western Europe was beginning to take shape as the Roman empire declined and Christianity became the accepted faith. I want to 'historicise': I think that what Augustine says about himself, God, language and narrative is easier to understand in context. His ideas about how texts can be written or read, and how people actually respond to written or spoken language, connect with recent critical theory, and I borrow some ideas which I hope to have understood, but there is a major difference.

Critical theory in the late twentieth century denies that there is an authoritative reading of any text, for neither the author nor the expert (critic or historian) can determine how any individual actually reads it. Augustine's account of his life can be read, as all texts can, in many ways. But he believes that there is an authoritative reading of his own and every life, known to God if not to him; that there is a canonical text, namely the Bible; and that there is a canon of interpretation, namely the fundamental beliefs of Christianity. Multiple readings, of a text or a life, are equally valid – provided they are all in accord with the basic truth.

Translations of Augustine and other authors are my own, because I wanted to keep as close as possible to the original. The Latin text of the *Confessions* is based on that of L. Verheijen OSA in *Corpus Christianorum*, series Latina 27, 1981. More elegant translations, and details of the text, are listed in the Guide to further reading.

Augustine habitually uses the masculine when speaking of God, but, fortunately, addresses God as 'you' throughout the *Confessions*; so I have not had to make the usual decision between masculine pronouns (for historical reasons) and inclusive language (for theological ones). For historical reasons, I have used the masculine in general references to fourth-century professional speakers and bishops. All dates are AD unless it is otherwise stated. References to the *Confessions* follow the usual convention of book number followed by both chapter and paragraph number (e.g. *C.*10.18.27). A few 'short title' references (e.g. Shaw, 'The family') are given in full in the Guide to further reading.

It is a sadness that J.P. Stern died just before the final draft of this Landmark was ready, so that it did not have the benefit of his comments. Professor E.J. Kenney brought about several improvements. My husband Stephen took time from his own work to comment on this. I owe a personal as well as an intellectual debt to Averil Cameron, Henry Chadwick and Robert Markus.

Chronology

(All dates are AD; some are approximate)

	Augustine's life	Political events	Church events
312		Constantine declares himself Christian	Donatist schism in Africa
324–337		Constantine ruler of the whole empire	
325			Council of Nicaea Eusebius, *History of the Church*
354	Birth of Augustine at Thagaste, N. Africa		
355			Conversion of Marius Victorinus
356			Death of St Antony of Egypt
361–3		Reign of Julian 'the apostate'	
366			Damasus bishop of Rome
c.370			Latin translation of Athanasius *Life of Antony*

fl.370s		Basil, Gregory of Nazianzus, Gregory of Nyssa
371	Augustine goes to university at Carthage	
372	Death of Augustine's father Patricius	
373		Ambrose consecrated bishop of Milan
375–6	Augustine begins to teach at Thagaste, then at Carthage	
378		Goths defeat the emperor Valens at Adrianople
379–95		Theodosius I ruler of the whole empire
c.380		Jerome begins work on the Vulgate
383	Augustine goes to Rome	
384	Augustine goes to Milan	
385		Jerome leaves Rome for the Holy Land
386	Augustine's conversion	
387	Death of Monica	
389		Paulinus of Nola baptised

390	Augustine returns to Africa; ? death of his son Adeodatus	
391	Augustine ordained priest at Hippo Regius	
392		Formal ban on pagan worship
394	Augustine lectures on Paul's Letter to the Romans	
395	Augustine consecrated as bishop of Hippo	Death of Theodosius: empire divided; Count of Africa revolts
c.397–401	Augustine writes the Confessions	
398		John Chrysostom bishop of Constantinople; Pelagius at Rome
c. 400		
406		Vandals invade France; Romans pull out of Britain
408		Theodosius II emperor in the east
410		Goths sack Rome
413–26	Augustine works on City of God	
418		Goths settle in Aquitaine
429		Vandals invade Africa
430	Death of Augustine	

Introduction

Take the books you wanted, my *Confessions*: look at me there so as not to praise me more than I am; believe what I say, not what others say, about me. Attend to me there and see what I was in myself and by myself. And if something in me pleases you, join me there in praising Him whom I wanted to be praised on my account − not me, for He made us, we did not make Him.   (Augustine, *Letter* 231.6)

Augustine wrote this late in his life in response to a letter from an admirer, and it helps to explain the purpose of the *Confessions* he had written years before, at the end of the fourth century. The English title 'confessions' puts us on the wrong track. We expect the story of an exciting and sometimes wicked life, and that is the element of the *Confessions* which attracts many readers: teenage gangs at Thagaste, disruptive students at Carthage, Augustine's sexual needs, his friend Alypius who was taken to a gladiator show and became addicted to bloodshed. But the Latin word *confessio* means something like 'acknowledging'. Augustine wrote the *Confessions* for people (some suspicious, some admiring) who wanted to know how a rising young professor of Latin rhetoric had come to be what he then was: a bishop who lived in celibacy and austerity, a spiritual not a political leader. He had the double purpose of acknowledging his own weakness and acknowledging the power of God manifested in his own life and in all creation. It is in this sense that his book is a confession, of sin, of faith and of praise. One man's life becomes a way of demonstrating true religion, and his experience displays the transformation of a culture.

The *Confessions* is often (and perhaps misleadingly) called 'the first autobiography'. But how can anyone, with or without precedent, describe his or her own life? What is to be selected or omitted, and how can the story be brought to an end when its subject goes on living? The point chosen as the conclusion, which 'closes' the narrative, determines the shape of the story. (For instance, 'Reader, I married him' is the closure of far too many stories about women; is there life after marriage?) Augustine seems to end his story in book 9, with his baptism as a Christian and the death of his mother who had constantly prayed for him – but then the *Confessions* goes on. To twentieth-century expectations (and probably to fourth-century expectations too) the *Confessions* is a puzzling work. The problem can be described in Augustine's own words: when he reread the *Confessions* (and all his other works) in his last illness, he noted that books 1–10 were about him, the other three about the creation narrative in the first verses of the Bible. He did not say why.

One provisional answer is that what interests him is the existence of a human being in relation to God. If the question is 'Who am I?', Augustine is not satisfied with the answer 'son of Patricius and Monica of Thagaste in Africa, formed by such and such a family and education, friends and books and experience'; he is a child of God, a prodigal son who squandered his inheritance, lived on pigswill, and came back at last to his home. He begins the story of his own life with the infancy he cannot remember, because that is where 'I' begin: he sees there the beginning of God's love and of human alienation from God. He selects events and stages of thought which map his journey away from home and from God, and the beginning of his return. He ends the story of his life perhaps fifteen years before the time of writing the *Confessions*, with his rebirth as a Christian and the death of his mother, who had been both a constant Christian presence and a tie to his former life.

Why, then, does the book not end where the life-story does? Again, I think, the answer is that what interests Augustine is the relationship between a human being and God. He reflects, in book 10, on what he has been doing in the *Confessions*, and asks how it has been possible for him to do it. How can the human mind recall the past, and how can he long for God without knowing God, who is beyond all human knowledge? He invokes God's help as he confesses not only his past errors, but his present faith and his partial understanding of the theological problems which had kept him outside the church: creation, incarnation, the existence of evil. In books 11 – 13 he interprets the first few verses of the Bible, using all the available techniques of multiple readings and hidden significance, to make sure his readers get their theology right, and do not (as he had done) think of God as good but powerless against evil, or as good and therefore remote from messy human existence.

The effect of the *Confessions* altogether, Augustine said when he reread them, was to arouse the human mind and emotions towards God. They did it so well that (unlike most texts of European literature) they survived the age of manuscript in many copies, just as Augustine's beloved Virgil did; they have shaped and interpreted the experience of Christians from the time of writing until now. But they also speak to readers who are not concerned with their lives, or with Augustine's, as focussed on God.

The *Confessions* is also called 'the first modern book'. 'Modern' is an unhelpful term, but it signals recognition of Augustine's self-awareness. What he says about himself is very different from earlier self-descriptions which survive from the Roman world, and often very close to the concerns of our own time. He describes emotionally charged relationships, with his mother, his friends, and above all with God. He combines vivid presentation and analysis with a sense that his own motives are beyond his intellectual reach: he is both fascinating and mysterious to himself, always dissatisfied with himself, and always aware of conflict and limitation. Books are as important as people in his life, and late twentieth-century readers recognise Augustine's awareness of himself as reader and writer and of his audience as readers, how language affects him and them, how a life can in practice, not only in the writing of autobiography, be shaped by fiction. Augustine is sure that without language, his own or that of others, there is no memory: he cannot retain, or pass on to others, what he cannot put into words. But a life can be 'read' differently at different times, and by choosing different words and different literary models to convey what is happening to us, we reinterpret not only our memories, but our experience now.

When Augustine first went to Carthage, aged seventeen, to begin his higher education, he tried out different interpretations of his longing and dissatisfaction. There was sexual desire for a partner, a wish to be 'in love' as in Virgil's account of Dido's love for Aeneas, or as it was more crudely presented in the Carthage theatre. There was also the love of wisdom, philosophy, described in the (lost) *Hortensius* of Cicero which Augustine read at the right age; in his later life, even though it is not a Christian text, he would often suggest it to clever people in search of God. The *Hortensius* inspired Augustine to seek further wisdom, and (since his mother had tried to bring him up a Christian) he turned to the Bible as an obvious source. But it was, at that stage of his life, such unsatisfying reading that he did not interpret his longing as the desire for God. The point can be briefly made in two quotations (not, in fact, used by Augustine):

> Sick with desire, and seeking him she loves,
> From street to street the raving Dido roves.
> So, when the watchful shepherd, from the blind,
> Wounds with a random shaft the careless hind,
> Distracted with her pain she flies the woods,
> Bounds o'er the lawn, and seeks the silent floods.
> (Virgil, *Aeneid* 4.68–73, in Dryden's adaptation)

Like as the hart desireth the waterbrooks, so longeth my soul after thee, O God; my soul is athirst for God, yea, even for the living God.
(Psalm 42, verses 1–2, as in the Book of Common Prayer 1662)

Virgil and the Bible are the texts which Augustine most often uses in the *Confessions* to interpret his life to himself: the masterpiece of the Latin classical canon and the canon of authoritative Christian Scripture. Which of them offered the true description of his state of mind when he began university at Carthage? The question is still in dispute. Some people agree with his own later diagnosis, that he failed to recognise his deepest desire for God because his head was full of popular romantic literature. Others think that he projected on to God feelings of desire and guilt which were sexual in origin. It depends what they think themselves about what matters in a human life. What was really happening to Augustine? It depends how his story, or anyone's story, ends; and none of us knows that.

Chapter 1

Augustine's world

1 Africa: world politics

Augustine was a local boy who made good, a provincial from an upland farm in the Roman province of Africa. This meant North Africa (present-day Morocco, Algeria, Tunisia and Libya), on the southern edge of the Roman empire which, in the late fourth century, still extended from Spain to the Euphrates and from the Rhine to the Sudan. Rome had ruled this huge territory for over three hundred years, but at a high cost. There were endless wars, on the frontiers and between rival claimants to power. Roman citizens were heavily taxed to pay for the armies which requisitioned their food, transport and labour. The supply of slaves was maintained by breeding, capture and kidnapping; many people who were not actually slaves were legally bound to an inherited trade or piece of land, so that they could not move away from danger or poverty. Strong emperors, like Constantine and Theodosius I, could hold the empire together, but the defence of most areas had to be left to powerful *duces* (leaders) and *comites* (Companions of the Emperor), the forerunners of mediaeval dukes and counts, who frequently decided that they could do better for themselves, and perhaps for their people, without imperial control. This happened in Africa twice in Augustine's lifetime; the result, again, was war.

The empire, even when politically united, was not a unity. The eastern empire, in Greece and Asia Minor and the Middle East, spoke Greek and looked to Constantine's new Christian capital, Constantinople, or to the ancient cities of Antioch and Alexandria. The western empire, in Italy and France and Spain, spoke Latin and was beginning to look away from Rome, the source of its traditions and home of its aristocracy, to the newer centres of Milan and Trier. Roman Africa belonged to the Latin west.

Africa and Rome

It is only a short sea-crossing from the province of Africa to Sicily, Italy or Spain, and in Augustine's time this link was more important than the journey eastwards to Greek-speaking Alexandria. The Arab conquest, which connected the North African coast to the Middle East as part of the Islamic world, came two centuries after his death. But the Middle Eastern connection was much older than that. The capital city of Roman Africa, Carthage, had originally been settled (in the eighth century BC) by Phoenicians from the Middle East. Carthage and Rome had fought three devastating Punic Wars (Punic from *Poeni*, the Latin for Phoenicians) which ended with Roman conquest in the mid-second century BC. Dialects of Punic were still spoken in country districts, and many people – including Augustine – understood a few words. But it was hard to find clergy who spoke anything other than Latin: churches began in the towns and urban culture was Latin.

There is no agreement about the survival of non-Roman culture in Africa: some scholars think that local Numidian culture flourished and was a factor in Christian schismatic movements. Augustine's mother Monica had a local, non-Roman, name, but her culture too was Latin, and he shows no awareness of himself as other than Roman, part of the dominant Mediterranean culture. It is sometimes suggested that, because he was African, he may have been black, and that he does not mention it because Romans took no particular notice of skin colour. Unfortunately, Romans did not lack colour prejudice – though it is quite true that they were just as rude about gangling red-haired Celts as they were about thick-lipped Ethiopians. A fourth-century collection of stories about the Desert Fathers (see 5) includes the black Father Moses of Scete, to whom the bishop said at his ordination 'Now you are all white.' 'But what am I inside?', asked Moses, and when his fellow clergy tested his humility by chasing out the 'black man' he reflected that they were right, for his skin was black as ashes. Augustine uses, unthinkingly, this association of black and badness: for instance, he reports (*City of God* 22.8) a woman's dream in which two 'curly-headed little black boys' turn out to be demons. If he had been black, could he have resisted the rhetorical contrast between his skin colour and his redemption from the devil? 'African', for him, means someone who lives in North Africa, and probably has the distinctive African accent; and in his time, Roman Africa looked north.

The fall of the western empire

Danger was also to come from the north. Central Asian tribes, moving (so far as anyone could see) quite unpredictably, displaced peoples whose names have become synonyms for ignorant destruction: Huns, Goths, Vandals. They moved across the Rhine and Danube into the empire, sometimes fighting against the armies of Rome, sometimes fighting for them in return for land. When Augustine was in the early years of his teaching career, in 378, the Goths defeated the then emperor only a little way from Constantinople. Not quite ten years after he wrote the *Confessions*, there was a mass movement of non-Romans across the Rhine, and the Roman government pulled its troops out of Britain to meet the threat. The year after that, in 410, Alaric the Goth besieged and sacked Rome. Many people saw this disaster as the end of an era, the final result of neglecting the gods of Rome for the Christian God.

Augustine did not see it like that. He knew his Roman history, an endless succession of wars and disasters survived; and even if this was the end of Roman power in the west, he saw no reason to think that any one empire was of particular importance. He did not live to see how the western empire, in the last decades of the fifth century, was replaced by kingdoms of Goths, Vandals, Franks and other 'barbarians' who claimed some continuity with Roman tradition; or how the Church, simply by surviving, became the preserver of the Latin language and of Roman culture. In 429, the year before his death, the Vandals crossed from Spain to Africa, killing and plundering. He had been bishop of Hippo Regius, on the coast, for thirty-five years: the town was under siege when he died.

His biographer Possidius records some of his last words, which came from two texts of major importance in his life (as they are in the *Confessions*). He recited the penitential psalms and quoted − in Latin adaptation − the philosopher Plotinus (see 5): 'The great man will not think it a great matter if sticks and stones fall and mortals die.'

2 Thagaste: family, church and school

In the small town of Thagaste in upland Numidia (now eastern Algeria), Augustine's childhood at least was safe from wars. He tells us (*C*.2.3.5) that his father Patricius was not rich. Patricius was not exactly poor either, since he was a *decurio*, a member of the local council of Thagaste; but this was an honour most men tried to avoid, as decurions were responsible for shortfalls in the tax-collection and were expected to help out the local budget. Patricius, who was not a Christian, had a devout Christian wife, Monica. There were at least three children. Augustine was probably the eldest; he had a brother, who appears without explanation at the deathbed of their mother (*C*.9.11.27), and a sister who never appears in the *Confessions*, who later became the leader of a community of Christian women. Sibling relationships simply do not feature in the *Confessions*: it is his friends and his mother who matter to Augustine, because he could talk to them about religion.

Patricius could afford to send his clever son away to school in the nearby town of Madaura. Schooling was not cheap. Parents negotiated with individual teachers, at whatever level, who expected presents as well as fees, and students needed an allowance. Then came a year which Augustine had to spend at home (*C*.2.3.5), getting into bad company, while his father (and some friends and relatives) found the money for his higher education at Carthage. Here, Augustine studied rhetoric and thought about religion, but did not return to the Christianity his mother had tried to teach him.

Latin Christianity

Roman Africa had a powerful tradition of martyrdom, religious conflict, and public denunciation of sinners: it has been called the Bible Belt of the Roman empire. Bishops were expected to preach every Sunday, expounding the Scriptures *ex cathedra*: that is, from a high-backed chair, the sign of status which dominated the church building as a professor's chair dominated the lecture hall or magistrate's the courtroom. So the cathedral church was the bishop's church. Many of the Christian laity came to church chiefly for the sermon, because they were not yet baptised and did not stay for the Eucharist. Baptism wiped out past sin, but many Christians (not only in Africa) did not see how they could be forgiven if they sinned after baptism. So they remained as catechumens, Christians under instruction, until they thought they could make the commitment. Augustine's father Patricius, who became a catechumen quite late in life, delayed baptism until his deathbed (so did the emperor Constantine and many others). Augustine's mother had made him a catechumen as a baby, and he wanted to be baptised as a child when he was very ill, but when he recovered she deferred his baptism (*C*.1.11.17). He was still a churchgoer when he went to Carthage — indeed, he picked up a girlfriend in church (*C*.3.3.5) — but he had not yet found any Christian preaching or writing of the intellectual level he needed.

Africa had been Latin-speaking for at least three hundred years before Augustine's birth, with a local tradition of elaborate rhetoric and a reputation for producing lawyers. Tertullian in the second century and Cyprian in the third were brilliant examples both of Latin rhetoric and of African Christianity; but Augustine seems not to have known their work when he was young. In particular, the old Latin Bible struck him as crude by comparison with the Virgil and Cicero he read at school. This was a real barrier for educated Romans after Constantine. At about the time when Augustine began teaching at Rome, in the early 380s, Bishop Damasus of Rome started Jerome on the task of producing a Latin Bible acceptable to the modern church. This far more accurate version, which we know as the Vulgate, did not simply improve the Latin style: Jerome went back to the Hebrew and Greek texts and did serious critical work on the tradition.

But the Vulgate created new problems, and met with the same chorus of disapproval as any English version which differs from the King James. When Augustine became a bishop, he used Jerome's version of the Gospels in his church at Hippo; but he wrote to Jerome (who was not pleased) to tell him how a local church had complained about the Old Testament. They did not like finding the prophet Jonah seated not under a gourd as he always had been, but under an ivy. Augustine thought this reaction revealed a more general problem: Jerome had undermined confidence in the Septuagint, the standard Greek translation of the Hebrew Old Testament. (Legend had it that the seventy − Latin *septuaginta* − translators, each working in isolation, had produced identical versions.) Augustine the intellectual could live with uncertainty, but Augustine the bishop knew the problems of those who could not.

There was brilliant theological writing in Augustine's youth, but the work of Basil, Gregory of Nazianzus and Gregory of Nyssa (the 'Cappadocian Fathers') was inaccessible to him because it was in Greek. Many people spoke Greek along the North African coast, but Augustine had to learn it at school and found it hard going. (Characteristically, he ascribed his difficulties to sinful disobedience, not to bad teaching methods: *C.*1.13.20.) Nor, evidently, were there any Christian intellectuals on hand in Thagaste and Madaura to inspire him. Augustine's mother, like most women of her time, had little education; she could only hope and pray and set an example, not argue with her brilliant son. So Augustine's adolescence was shaped by the great works of the classical literary tradition, above all the prose of Cicero and the poetry of Virgil.

Virgil and the classical curriculum

Primary school taught basic literacy and numeracy to both boys and girls. Boys who went on to a *grammaticus* expected to study a few classical authors, four or five hundred years

old, chosen for style rather than content. Virgil was unquestion-
ably the greatest Latin poet and Cicero the greatest writer of
prose, both political oratory and philosophical discussion; the
historian Sallust had a more 'pointed' style (and perhaps
African schoolboys liked his narrative of Rome's war with the
Numidian prince Jugurtha); the early dramatist Terence (himself
an African) wrote pure conversational Latin. These texts were
read with very close attention to grammar and vocabulary,
correctness of speech, choice and arrangement of words to
evoke a specific response, cultural allusions – everything that
would allow these schoolboys, in later life, to display their
own culture. The language of the classics was as far removed
from ordinary speech and pronunciation as Shakespeare is
from the language of schoolchildren now, and the *grammaticus*
had to spend time teaching his pupils how to read a text
written, after the Greek model, without word-divisions or
systematic punctuation, and in a Latin unlike the language they
actually spoke. It was all reinforced with beatings (*C*.1.9.14),
like a caricature of an old-style English public school (except
that the boys organised their own games). Nevertheless,
Augustine learned to love Virgil.

Every schoolboy knew the *Aeneid*, the epic poem (written
almost four hundred years earlier) which had both a literary
and a political programme. Virgil had set out to show that
Latin poetry could rival Homer and the Greeks, and that
Roman imperial rule was ordained by the gods and destined
to endure. His hero Aeneas experiences both the fighting of
Homer's *Iliad* and the search for home of Homer's *Odyssey*;
but the defining characteristic of Aeneas is not the fighting
skills of Achilles or the survival skills of Odysseus, but a
Roman devotion to duty and the will of the gods. The *Aeneid*
continued to be the charter-text of Roman education, even
when Christian emperors ruled and the worship of Virgil's
gods was actively discouraged. (When Augustine was a small
boy, some earnest Greek Christians had tried to compose
Christian alternatives to the standard classical texts, and the
equally earnest emperor Julian 'the apostate' had forbidden
Christians to teach a literature which, he said, they obviously

could not understand. Both attempts failed, and the classical curriculum survived.) But Augustine, like almost all young students of Virgil, was less impressed by the grandeur of Roman destiny than by the story of Dido queen of Carthage.

Dido's love for Aeneas almost diverts him from his destined task of founding Rome; it destroys her and puts her people at risk. Virgil gives more persuasive voices to the rage and suffering of Rome's (usually female) victims than he does to his Roman hero. Aeneas is obedient to Destiny, which is voiced by Jupiter, Father of gods and men. He leaves his ruined city carrying his aged father and leading his young son, a living image of Roman patriarchy, losing his wife Creusa whom he tells to follow at a distance. Destiny forbids him to become the consort of Dido, a refugee like himself, who is building the city of Carthage for her people: she sees their relationship as marriage, he does not; he is distressed by their parting, she commits suicide. This is, of course, a twentieth-century reading of Virgil. Augustine, a man of the fourth century, accepts patriarchy as part of the natural order. Yet he took from Virgil, and uses in the *Confessions*, images of destructive love, anguished parting, and the journey of an often bewildered man who seeks to interpret the Father's command.

3 Carthage: rhetoric and religion

Virgil was also a path to success. The schoolboy Augustine won high praise for composing and delivering a (prose) speech in which Juno, queen of the gods, rages at her inability to keep Aeneas out of Italy. Looking back, he saw it as dust and ashes (*C*.1.12.21): a false god, false emotions, praise for a meaningless achievement. But a further education in rhetoric, expensively bought at Carthage, was his family's investment for the future. The most obvious route into the imperial civil service was to be an advocate on the staff of the provincial governor, whose time was mostly taken up with lawsuits.

Augustine was now learning the 'liberal arts', literally the skills suitable for a free man, by contrast with the technical skills which might be exercised by slaves or wage-slaves who had to follow the master's orders. If a 'free man', that is someone who claimed to be a gentleman, wanted to study medicine or architecture or engineering, he did it as a form of philosophy, aiming to understand the workings of the physical world or the human body rather than to market his practical skills. 'Natural philosophy' survived into the nineteenth century as a name for what is now called science (though why that particular study should appropriate the Latin word for 'knowledge' is another question).

At school, Augustine had studied literature and begun rhetoric. He now added dialectic, the techniques of analysis and argument: this included the study of Aristotle's *Categories* (he found it quite straightforward and could not see why his tutor was so excited about it, *C*.4.16.28). More abstract analysis led to arithmetic and geometry and their applications in music and astronomy. These are the Seven Liberal Arts, the *trivium* and *quadrivium* inherited by mediaeval universities. It used to be said that Oxford 'Greats' (which no longer includes mathematics) produced people who always asked two questions: what do you mean, and how do you know? Augustine's higher education seems to have had the same effect on him, but it also had a practical aim.

Roman education was geared to producing expert speakers, just as twentieth-century education in 'the arts' has (until very recently) been geared to producing expert writers. Rhetoric, which for much of this century has been a term of disapproval ('mere rhetoric without content'), was the ability to make language do justice to the horror or glory of what was happening, and to inspire and persuade your hearers both by appropriate speech and by the right kind of argument. It required acute awareness of how language is used and how people respond, which was some justification for school training in the exact sense of words and the ability to deploy cultural allusions. Rhetoric also included memory training and the techniques of 'body-language' now taught by image-makers: gesture, eye-contact, breath-control, pitch and cadence of voice. It could take an unknown young man high in the service of the state. Augustine's family had planned (*C*.3.3.6) that he should be a lawyer; in fact he became a teacher of rhetoric. At the time when he decided to abandon his pursuit of success, ten years after he finished his own education, his teaching career had taken him from home to Carthage, then to Rome, and then to be Professor of Rhetoric at Milan.

Philosophy

But Augustine did not only want success: he wanted to lead a morally good life. One of his set books at Carthage (*C*.3.4.7) was the *Hortensius* of Cicero. He began to read it with an eye to style, but it was the content which impressed him. The *Hortensius* now survives only in quotations (many of them by Augustine), but we know that its explicit purpose was to encourage the study of philosophy. Philosophy means, literally, the love of wisdom, and this meant (for almost all Greek or Roman philosophers since Plato) the desire to understand God's design for the universe and for the human soul. It required not only intellectual effort, but invocation and contemplation of the divine, and a disciplined life which avoided distractions. This was *askēsis*, which means 'training' as for a race, and gave Christian asceticism its name; though some Christian ascetics, in Augustine's time, went in for extremes of renunciation and self-torment which non-Christian philosophers thought simply silly.

Plato, and the philosophers who followed him, directed attention away from this changeable world to the absolute good which, they believed, can be grasped by the exercise of reason. Human beings, they argued, are distinctively rational animals, and reason, which allows us to make sense of the world, is the aspect of humans which is closest to God. So intellectual work and prayer are not separate activities. The more we are committed to philosophy − the love of wisdom − the more we are like God, and we may eventually attain union with God, for our thoughts will not be other than God's thoughts. The further we are from God, the more fragmented we become, because we disperse our attention over the multiplicity and unreality of this world instead of focussing it on

God. Greed for pleasure or power, anger, sexual passion, are all distractions from what we ought to be doing. So the decision to follow philosophy could (at any time from the fourth century BC) amount to conversion, a radical change of lifestyle in favour of simplicity and study.

Augustine read the *Hortensius* at just the right age (he was nineteen) and remembered it all his life. He was a Christian, so (perhaps for the first time) he started to read the Bible for guidance on how he should live. But he found not only the style but the content disconcerting. If God made all that there is, did God make evil too? If God said 'Let us make man in our image', does that imply that God is like a human being? Are we really supposed to admire the patriarchs of Israel? 'Where does evil come from, and is God confined within a bodily form, and does God have hair and nails, and can men be called righteous when they have several wives at once, and kill people, and sacrifice animals?' (*C*.3.7.12).

Manichaeism

The questions were asked by missionaries of the Manichee religion which Augustine followed for the next nine years (*C*.4.1.4). Until quite recently, Manichaeism was known only from Christian polemic (much of it by Augustine in his later career), and it was difficult to see what could have been the attraction for intelligent people. But the discovery of Manichee texts, especially a book of psalms, has made it clearer.

Mani, the founder of Manichaeism, came perhaps from a Jewish sect in Mesopotamia, a meeting-point of religious traditions. He had tried (at some time in the third century) to formulate a universal religion which could spread east and west. He acknowledged Jesus as one of the prophets, but this entailed rejecting much of the New Testament as a false record of Jesus' life and teaching — in particular the claim that he underwent death on the cross. Mani taught a form of Gnosticism, the belief that a few choice spirits, imprisoned in this corrupt and deceptive world, escape from delusion and have knowledge (*gnosis*) of the truth: which is that the universe is a perpetual battle between Good or Light, which is dispersed and entrapped in the material world, and the invasive power of Evil or Darkness. Everything that happens in the world and in an individual life can be explained as an aspect of this struggle. The hope of those who have seen the light is to be freed from the lower nature which keeps them in this world.

'Manichaean', in Christian polemic, still means an insistence on seeing things in black and white, and a refusal to accept that the world and human bodily existence, though flawed by sin, is God's good creation. The Manichee Elect were celibate and followed strict dietary rules which were supposed to help them liberate trapped particles of Good (melons and cucumbers had a particularly high light content). This concern for food provides Augustine with one of the dominant images of *Confessions* 3 and 4: the inadequate spiritual food supplied by Manichaeism, and the inventions of classical literature, are like the 'husks that the swine did eat', the garbage which the Prodigal Son was reduced to eating when he left his father's house and wasted his inheritance (Luke 15.16). 'I was far away in a foreign country, shut out from you and from the husks of the pigs whom I was feeding on husks' (*C*.3.6.11).

Manichee 'Hearers', supported by the prayers of the Elect, had a less restricted lifestyle, but were told to remain faithful to one partner and to avoid procreating more human beings, since that would entrap more spirits in matter. Augustine became a Hearer, and we have to ask why. The answer is probably that Manichaeism could explain everything: in particular, it could assure him that behaviour he disliked in himself was caused by evil influences outside his true self (*C*.5.10.18), and it offered a solution to the problem of where that evil came from. The 'problem of evil', as usually stated, is that if God is omnipotent, God must be responsible for evil, either by having brought it into being, or by allowing it to continue. But if God is love, God would do neither. Mani's solution was to give up omnipotence. If Evil is an independent force, which can be resisted but not overcome by Good, then God is not to be blamed either for creating evil or for allowing evil to continue.

There were other attractions besides those of doctrine. Manichees had imposing, beautifully written and decorated texts, full of the True Wisdom in suitably mysterious form, far more impressive than the Latin Old Testament which they encouraged Augustine to dismiss. They also had a strong supportive network which was hidden from all but the true believers. Manichaeism was politically suspect, as any association might be, but especially because it came from Mesopotamia and therefore might be a fifth column of Rome's major enemy, the Sassanid Persian empire. Manichees infiltrated Christian congregations but did not declare themselves. This must have been exciting: they could feel that they were on the edges of danger, but in the secret of the movement and the truth.

Gradually Augustine discovered that the Manichees of Carthage were not as profound as he had thought. When he asked a difficult question, they resorted to myths and metaphors, and assured him that everything would be explained when the great Faustus came. The Manichee hierarchy was (deliberately) similar to the Christian, and Faustus was their bishop of Rome. Eventually, when Augustine was twenty-nine, he did come to Carthage, and he was charming, but a disappointment (C.5.6.10−7.12). He was not nearly as well read as Augustine in the liberal arts, and that was not his only lack.

Astrology

Augustine had also been reading widely in natural philosophy. He could not see how to reconcile the calculations of astronomers with Manichee stories of the sun, moon and stars; and Faustus admitted that neither could he. This problem had practical implications, because Augustine was, like many men of his time, very interested in astrology. It seemed obvious that the stars belonged to a higher and more ordered level of being than our own and that horoscopes could be properly scientific predictions in a dangerous world; moreover, astrology could shift the blame for wrongdoing away from the individual and on to cosmic forces (C.4.3.4). Astrologers were called *mathematici* and could make a living from their skill (at some risk, because aspiring politicians also wanted to know their future and the astrologer could find himself accused of fostering rebellion or crime). Augustine had a distinguished friend, Vindicianus, who had studied astrology as a profession until he decided it was a bogus science and transferred to medicine (*C*.4.3.5).

Augustine finally lost confidence in astrology, years later (he does not say exactly when), because his friend Firminius (*C*.7.6.8) produced a counter-example. Firminius had been born at exactly the same time as a slave child in a nearby house. His father and the slave's owner were so interested in astrology that they cast horoscopes even for domestic animals. So they knew that the two children had identical horoscopes – but their lives were as different as might be expected for the son of the house and a slave.

4 Africa to Italy: Manichees and pagans

When Augustine left Carthage for Rome (after a period of teaching in his home town), he was already dissatisfied with Manichee mythology, but was still convinced by their rejection of the Old, and much of the New, Testament. He thought (*C*.5.10.19–20) that Christians held a crudely anthropomorphic belief about God, and that Manichee teaching was more spiritual even though it treated Good and Evil as material substances. But there was still the problem of evil. Augustine's friend Nebridius had produced a devastating argument (*C*.7.2.3). What would happen if God did not bother to fight evil? If evil could actually damage God, then God is corruptible, and so are those fragments of God which (according to Manichee belief) are trapped in the material world and especially in human beings: what kind of God is that? If evil could not damage God, what is the point of the great Manichee struggle? Augustine was inclined to suspend judgement, following the 'Academic' school of philosophy which held that there is no conclusive proof of anything.

In the meantime, he used his Manichee contacts. He stayed in the house of a fellow-Hearer at Rome, and the Manichee

connection helped him to the chair of rhetoric at Milan
(C.5.13.23). Symmachus, the prefect of Rome who made
the appointment, was a 'pagan', an adherent of the traditional
Roman religion. 'Pagan' may be an army term for the 'civvies'
who did not serve in the army of Christ, or it may mean 'the
backwoods' because country people kept their traditions long
after the towns were officially Christian. In practice, many of
those whom Christians called pagans were intelligent and
high-minded people, who saw the ancient rites both as an
important aspect of social cohesion, and as a 'coded' version
of the hidden truths about God expounded by the great
philosophers. (Some present-day theologians take much the
same view of church-going.) Symmachus was one of these,
and was engaged in a political and religious power struggle
with Bishop Ambrose of Milan. He had no wish to strengthen
Ambrose's hand by appointing a Christian to a conspicuous
public post.

5 Milan: worldly success and renunciation

Augustine tells us that each of the departures in his teaching
career, from Thagaste, Carthage and Rome, had some immediate emotional or practical motive. Thagaste became
unbearable after the death of a friend (C.4.7.12), the students
at Carthage were disruptive (C.5.8.14), the students at Rome
cheated their teachers out of fees (C.5.12.22). But each move
was also a step up the ladder, from small town to provincial
capital to the heart of empire. Rome was the ancient centre of
empire and culture, but Milan was the emperor's Italian base:
it was nearer the major army routes from France to the Balkans
and better placed to respond to the endless movements of the
northern tribes. Augustine's duties included 'panegyrics'
(C.6.6.9), formal and (he says) quite untrue speeches of praise
which advertised the achievements and intentions of the
emperor. He might reasonably hope (C.6.11.19) to end as
governor of at least a minor province, if he married a wife
with money and made good use of his contacts. (He was not
likely to be sent back to Africa: its importance as a supplier

of grain required a senior man.) It may seem an odd way to choose a provincial governor, but in the nineteenth and early twentieth centuries much of the British empire was governed by young men who had demonstrated their ability by writing Greek and Latin prose and verse and by reading Demosthenes and Cicero. Macaulay defended this practice with the argument that, whatever the educational system, the man who showed the greatest ability would be the best public servant.

Can the good man serve the state?

But, in the late fourth century, the most high-minded public servants needed convincing that they ought to stay in their jobs. Ever since the days of Plato and Socrates, it had been argued that the cares of householding and government obstructed the pursuit of wisdom, but that the 'wise man' would do his duty to his family and his city. Christians were unconvinced: the New Testament encouraged them to think of fellow-Christians as their true family, and themselves as citizens of another country, temporary residents in a world which could not last. This caused no major problems while Christianity was a minority religion. But Constantine, only thirty years before Augustine's birth, had made Christianity an officially approved, state-subsidised religion of the empire; and Theodosius I, who became emperor when Augustine was twenty-five, put increasing pressure on those who tried to maintain the old religion (though in practice he appointed the most suitable men he could find for any given job).

The main functions of Roman imperial government were defence and law enforcement. Christians accepted the commandment 'Thou shalt not kill', together with Jesus' teaching that they must turn the other cheek: they were instructed not only to refrain from murder but to meet violence with non-violence. How then could they be soldiers, or give soldiers the order to kill, or enforce the law by its usual methods of torture (supposedly to establish the truth), physical punishment for those who had nothing else to lose, and execution? Christian tradition had been formed in three centuries when there were always other people to serve in the army and exercise justice. It was extremely difficult to reconcile Christian pacifist teachings with the requirements of law and defence: some Christians have always said it is impossible. Augustine's own conversion to Christianity came when he was perhaps a few years away from becoming governor of a province, with the authority to order criminals to be tortured and executed, and necessary involvement (even in the civil service) in financing and supplying the troops.

But the use of force was not the only problem for people who wanted to lead good lives. Augustine had brought friends with him to Milan (*C*.8.6.13), young professional men like him, fellow-Africans trying to establish themselves in metropolitan careers and wondering if they were doing the right thing. Alypius was a lawyer, unemployed after three terms as a legal assessor 'selling advice'. Augustine himself was a 'word-salesman' (*C*.9.5.13), a professional speaker and teacher, though he was not sure that rhetoric can be taught. Nebridius was teaching literature as assistant to another friend, Verecundus. They were all engaged in perpetuating a system and a culture about which they had serious doubts, and they spent all the time they could in reading and discussing philosophy and theology. They were on the fringes of the Church; some of their best friends were Christians, and so were some of the men they most admired.

Ambrose and Platonism

Bishop Ambrose of Milan was a Roman aristocrat, trained in philosophy and rhetoric, who had been the governor of this important district before its people demanded him for bishop. He had been kind to Augustine on his arrival (*C*.5.13.23). Augustine went to hear him preach, interested at first only by his rhetorical skill, but coming to realise (*C*.5.14.24−5) that Ambrose could interpret even the most off-putting sections of the Old Testament to show their spiritual value. Ambrose did this by using the same technique as his 'pagan' opponents used to interpret their rituals and the accounts of gods in Homer:

he treated Scripture as allegory, a system of coded references to profound truths about God and the universe. He often cited the words of Paul: 'the letter kills, but the spirit gives life' (*C*.6.4.5). In his *Hexaemeron* (the Six Days of Creation), sermons on Genesis which Augustine may well have heard, he challenged the Manichee interpretation of 'let us make man in our image'. It was, he said, the human soul, not the human body with its physical senses and passions, which was in God's image. He also attacked the Manichee doctrine of the 'alien nature' which was responsible for evil, borrowing arguments from the philosopher Plotinus. It was the first time Augustine had heard Christianity expounded at this intellectual level.

The Manichee arguments against Christianity now looked as unconvincing as other parts of their teaching, and Augustine decided that he could no longer be a member of the sect. His mother had come to join him at Milan, and her devotion encouraged his interest in Christian practice; he went regularly with her to hear Ambrose preach. But he could not yet declare himself a committed Christian: his real concern was for the philosophy which Ambrose used so effectively in his sermons.

There was a group of Milan intellectuals who met to study Platonist philosophy. One of them gave Augustine 'Platonist books' in Latin translation (*C*.7.9.13). He does not say what exactly the books were: probably some works by the third-century philosopher Plotinus, who had taught in Rome, and perhaps some by his student Porphyry, who had organised Plotinus' unsystematic treatises in *Enneads* (groups of nine) to make them more accessible to readers. There was a common Platonist tradition, though there were (of course) differences of interpretation within it. This 'late Platonism' is often called Neoplatonism, but the philosophers concerned were quite sure that they were not innovating, but correctly expounding the implications of Plato's philosophy.

The *Confessions* show which Platonist arguments made the greatest impact on Augustine. He had not wanted to think of God in human form, but did not know how to think of God except in images of something physical which occupies space. Platonist texts directed his attention to the great power of the mind which forms these images, but does not occupy space (*C*.7.1.1–2). The problem which still preoccupied him was the origin of evil: the Platonist texts he read argued that there is no independent power of evil which sets out to challenge God. Corruption can only make sense (*C*.7.12.18) as the corruption of something originally good, which has turned or fallen away from God. Everything owes its existence to God, so something which is utterly corrupt ceases to exist. Apparent evils are really conflicts of interest (as it might be, mine and a female mosquito's), or part of the workings of the universe (like floods and volcanic eruptions), or the consequence of bad choices.

But why should anything turn or fall away from God? Plotinus considered the possibility that it is by a free choice, a kind of self-assertiveness. What really matters is that, finding ourselves to have fallen away into the 'region of unlikeness' (the phrase comes from Plato, and Augustine uses it in *C*.7.10.16), we can climb back to higher things by the ascent of reason. We must 'go into ourselves', reflect on our own thinking and how we make sense of the world, and think what must be true for this activity to be possible. Eventually we may attain union with God, in that our thoughts will (for a moment) be the same as the thoughts of God, not multiple and successive as they usually are. Augustine tried to do what Plotinus taught, to 'lift the mind's eye' up to God (*C*.7.3.5), but always fell back. 'I could not stand firm to enjoy my God, but I was caught up to you by your beauty and wrenched away from you by my weight, and crashed groaning down into lesser things: and that weight was my sexual habit' (*C*.7.17.23).

Marriage or celibacy?

There was another choice to be made in the pursuit of wisdom. Augustine and his friends were uncertain whether they should continue their careers or devote their lives to study and prayer (*C*.6.14.24). If they married, they would have a household and children to support, and their wives might reasonably object (*C*.9.3.5) to their renouncing worldly concerns. If they did not marry, both Christians and non-Christian philosophers taught that they should live in chastity. It was argued that the only proper use of sex is within marriage for the procreation of children, and that any other use is lust, which damages the soul.

Augustine had been living with a woman since he was a student at Carthage (*C*.4.2.2); they had a son, Adeodatus (the name means 'God's gift'), an unplanned but much loved child. But Augustine's future career depended on finding a wife of good family with money of her own. His mother was negotiating a suitable marriage − but this meant (see 10) that he had to send away his long-term partner. He found it impossible to manage without a temporary substitute, whose attraction was not long-standing affection, but sex. Chastity, he thought, was beyond him. Meanwhile, he found his job stressful. He makes a rather trite contrast (*C*.6.6.9) with the immediate happiness of a drunken beggar, but improves on it by suggesting that he was in a state of permanent, but depressed, intoxication by worldly fame. He was also confronted by examples of people who had achieved what he could not in philosophy.

Platonism and Christianity

Porphyry's biography of Plotinus described a man who 'seemed ashamed of being in a body' and who (like Porphyry himself on one occasion) had several times reached the height of contemplation, the point at which his thoughts were not distinct from the thoughts of God. Augustine could not do this, and had some doubts about Platonist philosophy altogether (*C*.7.20.26). Eventually (*C*.8.1.1) he went to seek advice from Simplicianus, a friend of Ambrose, and said he had been reading Platonist texts. Simplicianus told him (*C*.8.2.3) the story of Marius Victorinus who had translated them. This man was another African, a teacher of rhetoric and a philosopher so distinguished that his statue was in the Forum at Rome. He had taught at Rome in the time of Constantine and had come to accept Christianity after years of opposition. The

Roman clergy offered to let him make his profession of faith
in private, to avoid embarrassment, but he made it before the
congregation, all of whom knew him and rejoiced (*C*.8.2.5).
Augustine wanted to follow his example, but he felt (*C*.8.5.12)
like someone who wants to get up but is overcome by the
pleasure of sleep, and murmurs 'Yes, in a minute'.

Augustine 'seized on' the apostle Paul (*C*.7.21.27) as a
corrective to the Platonist books. Paul insisted that people
must acknowledge their sinfulness and that only God's free
gift − what Christians call grace − can liberate them from the
compulsion to sin. By contrast, non-Christian philosophers
seemed to rely too arrogantly, or too optimistically, on human
reason as a route to God. Augustine says he can remember
(*C*.7.20.26) the impact the Platonist books made on him
before he read the Scriptures; he thinks it was meant that he
should read them that way round, so that he could see the
difference 'between presumption and confession'.

Augustine told, in book 6 of the *Confessions*, the story of
his friend Alypius, who was frankly puzzled by Augustine's
enjoyment of sex (*C*.6.12.21) but had a comparable problem.
Alypius was addicted to violence − not inflicting it, but seeing
it inflicted at 'the games'. Roman games included fights to the
death between men and animals (the more savage and exotic,
the more popular) or between trained fighters. Intelligent
Romans found enjoyment of them as repellent as an addiction
to snuff movies; the emperor Constantine had banned gladiator
fights, but it took another two centuries for the ban to be
properly enforced. Alypius had managed to kick the habit
when he was a student at Carthage, but had succumbed again
at Rome when some friends dragged him along to a gladiator
show. He told them they could take him but not make him
watch (*C*.6.8.13), so he sat with his eyes shut. But he did not
stop his ears; a roar from the crowd made him open his eyes,
and one look was enough. He was addicted again, despite all
his principles, until 'much later' God rescued him.

Reason had not been enough for Alypius or for Augustine;
Paul thought that moral law was actually counter-productive,
making people more aware of what was forbidden and more

eager to do it (Romans 7.7–8). By the time Augustine wrote the *Confessions*, he had decided that the solution is not to oppose reason and desire — 'I want to do this, but I ought not to' — but to acknowledge the deepest desire, which is for God. Then the love of God can overcome lesser loves: I want to do this, but there is something I want more. It becomes possible, as he put it in his *Treatises on John's Gospel*, to 'love, and do what you will' (one of Augustine's most misunderstood sayings). The weight of sexual desire which pulled Augustine down from the heights of contemplation became (*C*.13.9.10) the weight of love which pulled him into his proper place, as a body settles to rest. But, looking back on his time at Milan, he was chiefly aware of compulsion and frustration, the gulf between his human nature and God.

Platonist philosophers argued that God's unchanging love permeates and orders the universe, and inspires those who achieve the higher levels of contemplation, but (*C*.7.9.13) they did not offer Christ as the mediator between human nature and God. It is one of the greatest puzzles of the *Confessions* that Augustine does not give more time to the differences between Platonism and Christianity, or to his study of Christian doctrine in preparation for baptism. Perhaps he would have found it impossible to discuss this without writing several more books; or perhaps the fact was that he had not realised, at the time of his baptism, the nature of the problem. Fourth-century Christians had not yet formulated a definition of how Christ could be fully God and fully human; Alypius, in fact, had thought the official doctrine was that Christ was 'only God and flesh', without a human mind. Both he and Augustine had thought it obvious from the New Testament (*C*.7.19.25) that Christ was a fully human being, of exceptional wisdom, who experienced human temporal existence (at one time he is doing this, at another something else) and human suffering: physical pain, grief, fear, death. But Augustine wanted (*C*.7.3.4) a God who is not subject to corruption or to change.

Emotion, in the philosophical tradition, was thought of as vulnerability: the Greek word *pathos* means experience, suffering, illness as well as emotion. Emotions, as it were, come from outside and hit you, and you may succumb. But Plato had argued that God is perfect goodness and therefore not subject to change, because any change would have to be for the worse. So there was a problem about God in the Old Testament manifesting anger (somebody's wrongdoing had, so to speak, got to God), or deciding to spare a condemned city (had God been wrong to condemn it?); and also about Christ experiencing fear in the garden of Gethsemane and, worst of all, death on the cross. It seemed that what has to be true of a human being (genuine uncertainty, suffering, death) cannot also be true of God. How could a Platonist accept the incarnation?

But the problem which looms largest in the *Confessions* is creation. The very first words of the Bible are 'In the beginning God created the heavens and the earth'. Could there be such a beginning? Genesis seems to suggest that God decided, at a particular moment in time, to create the universe. If so, had God allowed a less good state of affairs to prevail before the creation, or a worse one afterwards? And surely God must change, in that there must be a difference between God before creating the universe and God after creating the universe, and indeed in that God knows the succession of changing events in the created universe, so God's knowledge changes. Augustine's solution in *Confessions* 11 is to reject the language of 'before' and 'after': time, he says, depends on change, because it is a measure of the relationship between objects and events which exist in succession in the created universe. God created time but does not exist in time (see 12); everything is present to God without variation or sequence. This generates new problems, because, if everything is eternally present to God, all possibilities must be fixed: it is already certain that I shall, or shall not, escape from sin. All these difficulties were linked with the basic Christian belief that God does take initiatives for the benefit of human beings, showing mercy for their sins and finally reconciling God and humanity in the person of Christ; but Augustine seems much more concerned about creation than about incarnation.

Conversion

Augustine's intellectual position changed (see 14), but the decision he saw as critical for his conversion was that of living in chastity and renouncing the marriage which would have financed his ambitions. It was prompted (*C*.8.6.13ff.) by another of the apparently chance happenings which (in retrospect) shaped his life. Another fellow-African, a court officer called Ponticianus, dropped in on him and Alypius because he wanted a favour. He picked up a book which lay on a gaming-table: it was not a textbook on rhetoric, but the letters of Paul.

Ponticianus, a Christian who had a profession and a family, told them the story of two members of the secret police. These men had been working at the western capital Trier when they encountered a community of monks – something new for the western empire in the mid-fourth century. In Egypt, perhaps a century earlier, Christians had begun to abandon their property – and the distracting social and family duties which went with it – to live in the desert as solitaries (*monachoi*) or in communities dedicated to prayer. The stories and experience of these Desert Fathers inspired westerners to follow suit, rather as, in the 1960s, westerners inspired by Indian spiritual tradition 'dropped out' from conventional careers. The monks at Trier had a copy of the life of St Antony of Egypt. It inspired the secret policemen to renounce their profession and join the monks: why, they asked, should they manoeuvre to stay in the emperor's favour, when they could become friends of God for the asking? Their fiancées followed their example and chose virginity; their married friends turned sadly back.

This story made Augustine painfully conscious of all the years in which he had postponed his search for wisdom in favour of worldly success and sexual pleasure, praying, in effect, 'give me chastity and continence, but not yet' (*C*.8.7.16). He was still unable to make the break with his past life until he was liberated by divine intervention. He heard a voice 'like a child's' calling 'Take and read'; and what he read in Paul was a verse exhorting chastity (see further 14). He was now able to abandon his wish for marriage and for worldly success (*C*.8.12.30).

The rest of the story is told with surprising speed. Augustine resigned his chair unostentatiously (*C*.9.2.2–4) at the end of term, pleading ill-health, and went to stay in Verecundus' country house at Cassiciacum with Alypius and a group of family and friends. There he read the Psalms and argued with Alypius about Christ (*C*.9.4.7–8). At the end of the vacation he went back to Milan and was baptised with Alypius and with his son Adeodatus, whom he thought capable of so early a commitment. They joined up with Evodius (*C*.9.8.17), also from Thagaste, who had also renounced his profession (another repentant secret policeman), and decided to go back to Africa. At Ostia, while they waited for a passage home, Augustine and Monica shared a very Platonist vision; soon after, Monica died and was buried, not in her homeland – but she had come to realise (*C*.9.11.27–8) that it was not important to die with African ritual. (Her burial place at Ostia was discovered in 1945 by two boys digging a hole for their basketball post.) Augustine does not describe the year he spent in Rome, waiting until the sea-crossing was safe after yet another civil war. In the event, he returned to Africa after only five years away. Milan had been geographically and spiritually the furthest point of his journey.

6 Return to Africa: monks and bishops

The *Confessions* does not explain what happened after Monica's death, and the story has to be reconstructed from other writings. Back in Thagaste, Augustine formed a small community of friends in his family's house: it was probably the first monastery in the province. But, like many other would-be monks (including, in the fourth century, Saints Basil and John Chrysostom) he was pressed into a different kind of public service.

Each city or town or even large village in the empire had its bishop, who was a community leader as well as a preacher. In New Testament times, 'bishop' (from Greek *episkopos*, 'supervisor') was one of several possible titles for the people in authority in a Christian congregation. As the Christian churches reacted to doctrinal difference and to occasional persecution, it became standard practice to have one bishop as the leader and spokesman of a congregation; bishops in a given area would meet to decide policy. The local bishop became a public figure, especially when Constantine declared his support for Christianity: he gave bishops the power to settle local disputes, and they were expected to use their contacts and influence to help their people. When Constantine summoned the first ecumenical Church council to meet at Nicaea in 325, the assembled bishops declared that men of high social status should not be hastily ordained, for even if they were natural leaders by worldly standards, what the church needed was men with long experience of prayer and the Christian life. But local churches often saw it otherwise. The people of Milan had demanded Ambrose the governor for their bishop; and when Augustine visited a friend at the seaport of Hippo (which he thought was safe because it already had a bishop), its bishop alerted the congregation to the talent in their midst. Augustine was forcibly ordained priest, and (according to his biographer Possidius) when he wept for the loss of his monastic life, they thought he was crying from rage that he could not be bishop at once.

Bishops could not renounce the world. Ambrose, Augustine's exemplar, did not believe in keeping the church out of politics. He affirmed its moral authority to judge even the emperor, and once excluded Theodosius from communion for authorising the massacre of innocent people. He was endlessly busy with arbitrations: Augustine did not dare interrupt his brief leisure (which he used for refuelling with food and study) with a plea for theological discussion (C.6.3.3). Augustine himself, as bishop of a small coastal town, was drawn back into the world of lawsuits and contacts, pulling strings (for instance) to find out the exact state of the law on slavery and to get it enforced against illegal trading. He found himself pleading with judges and commanders to stay in their jobs, exercising what mercy they could and refraining from anger and hatred in the task of preserving the civil peace. In wrestling with his people's need for defence against invasion and protection against crime,

Augustine produced the greatest ever work of Christian political philosophy, the *City of God* — but that is another landmark.

Augustine had had three years in his monastic community: during this time his son had died, aged eighteen. There is nothing to say whether his brother and sister were important in his life at Thagaste. Then came his visit to Hippo and his forced ordination. From then on he lived, still in a small community of men, in a clergy house with a garden beside the cathedral. Preaching was the bishop's job, but Augustine was asked to do it even when he was a priest — not just at Hippo, but at the provincial synod when the local clergy met. Bishop Valerius of Hippo did not want to lose him, and as soon as he could (perhaps five years later) arranged for Augustine to be ordained assistant bishop with the right to succeed him. This was, strictly speaking, irregular, but Valerius probably did not know that — the canons (i.e. decisions) of supposedly ecumenical councils, including Nicaea, were not always widely publicised or even accurately translated.

Augustine's consecration as bishop confronted him with his past. People remembered his Manichee connection and were not convinced that he had broken it. They had no proof of his baptism at Milan, and Ambrose had not asked his home church for letters attesting his fitness. The rival Donatist church was ready to use any weapon against him. North African Christians were divided, very much as Northern Ireland is today, for historical and theological reasons which were often scarcely understood but were a pretext for feuding. When Constantine became emperor and the persecution of Christians ended, some Christians (named from one of their leaders, Donatus) argued that anyone who had given way, even to the extent of surrendering copies of the Bible to the police, was a source of contamination to the 'gathered church' of the righteous. The new bishop of the Catholic (i.e. universal) church in Carthage had, they said, been consecrated by one of these 'betrayers', and they chose a rival bishop of what they considered to be the true church. The schism continued and worsened. Catholics were the minority church in Hippo and in much of North Africa. Families and communities were divided between Catholics and Donatists: Augustine's mother had Donatist relatives. The Donatists had a paramilitary wing, the Circumcellions, but murder, maiming and lynching were committed by both sides. Government intervention repeatedly failed.

Augustine, in his first years as bishop, had to demonstrate both that he had rejected Manichaeism and that Donatism was theologically wrong in excluding sinners from the church. He wrote extensively on both subjects, at all levels from public controversy to academic debate; meanwhile, he had to keep up his preaching and pastoral work for an ordinary congregation in a modest provincial town, act as theological consultant to a province, and respond to intelligent Christians or non-Christians in search of discussion, feeling all the time that he had come late to Christianity and that he was still in constant need of God's help. In the midst of all this, he wrote the *Confessions*.

Chapter 2

Genre: describing a life

7 'The first ten books are about me ...'

What kind of book is the *Confessions*? As you begin to read, the answer is not obvious. Augustine starts from his impulse to praise God: 'You rouse us so that it delights us to praise you, because you made us for yourself, and our heart is restless until it is at rest in you' (*C*.1.1.1). Immediately, he has a problem to put to God. Which comes first, invoking God or praising God? Is it possible to invoke God unless you first know God? How do you know whom you are invoking? He finds an answer: calling upon God is itself an act of belief in God. But this raises more problems. To invoke (Latin *invocare*) is to call in: how can Augustine call 'in' God, who made heaven and earth? Into what, and from where? Augustine would not exist if God were not in him, or rather if he were not in God; and how can there be any place where God is not? God has said (in the book of the prophet Jeremiah) 'I fill heaven and earth': what exactly does this mean?

Here, you might reasonably think, is a very intelligent and philosophically aware person trying to understand what he is doing, which is praising God. The dominant questions of the first chapters are 'What are You?' and 'Who am I?'. Augustine says (*C*.1.6.7) 'I do not know where I came from', and moves, abruptly, to what seems to be the beginning of human life, the infancy which he cannot remember but can reconstruct from his parents' stories and from watching other babies (including, no doubt, his own son). The rest of book 1 reflects on his infancy and childhood as manifestations of human greed, disobedience and social corruption (see 9). It is extraordinarily vivid but also detached from any particular context. Only at *Confessions* 2.3.5 is there, suddenly, a local habitation and a name: Augustine's father Patricius, a modest family from Thagaste, school at Madaura, plans for education at Carthage.

Is this autobiography? Books 1–9 of the *Confessions* follow the same overall pattern as the opening chapters. There is a chronological sequence from infancy to death – that is, the death of Augustine's mother Monica, which comes soon after his abandonment of his former life and his rebirth as a Christian. Every so often Augustine tells us where we are now (Carthage, Rome, Milan, Ostia), how old he is, what students he is teaching, but these mentions are always very brief. He recalls books he read and conversations he had, but what he spends time on is the beliefs he held about God, the reasons why he held them, and the questions they raise. He tries out and discards ideas as in a philosophical treatise. 'Is this the answer? but, if so ...', always referring the question to God and accompanying it with acknowledgement of his own faults, appeals for further understanding, and praise.

So the *Confessions* is intellectual or spiritual autobiography. (There is no real difference, because Augustine's spiritual and intellectual life cannot be separated.) It is the record of what a very intelligent man thought about God at different times of his life, made more convincing because we can imagine the person he was when he held these beliefs, but it is not concerned with other aspects of his life. To make a biography which fits twentieth-century expectations (as in Peter Brown's *Augustine of Hippo*), the outline narrative which can be found in the *Confessions* has to be filled out and the settings described, often from other writings of Augustine himself. But that does not answer all the questions raised by the *Confessions*. Autobiographies often end with some decisive moment – commitment to a career, a marriage, a philosophy – at some distance from the author's present lifestyle, which may not seem to him or her very interesting. That would explain why the narrative (such as it is) of Augustine's life ends at book 9 as he waits to return to Africa after his mother's death. But what do we make of the remaining books? Augustine said that books 1–10 are about him. What is the function of book 10, and why should he add three books of biblical exegesis?

Is the 'Confessions' a unity?

All kinds of narrative patterns have been found in the *Confessions*, but it is a widely held opinion that the *Confessions* has no overall plan. Many critics think that Augustine initially wrote an autobiography (books 1–9) ending with the decisive year of his conversion and his mother's death. The end of book 9 is a valediction to Monica and the *Confessions* together, and can be read as a dedication of the work, saying in effect 'in memory of my parents, who brought me into this life, and especially my mother who saw me a Christian before she died'. His readers wanted more, so he added book 10 to answer, or fend off, questions about his present life. Books 11–13 are an appendix; and people who think this often admit that they do not know why these books are there. This seems very unsatisfactory. You need a reason for an appendix, and the reason is usually that the appendix contains material too boring or too technical to fit in the main text. But Augustine was quite passionately interested in the content of books 11–13, and if they were too technical to fit with an autobiography, he could have used the material in other theological writings.

Perhaps it is a mistake to think of 'adding books of exegesis'. If the *Confessions* is spiritual autobiography, then Augustine's present theological position is obviously relevant – or, more strongly, is the whole point. He might be writing apologia, an explanation of how he came to hold his present beliefs and a defence against those who suspected him of holding others. Or he might (Courcelle, *Recherches*) be using a technique of evangelism which he recommended for converts undergoing instruction. His strategy was to show at least some of the wonderful things God had done in this one human life, by dreams, visions, interventions of one kind or another; then, having established the point that God is active in human lives, he could expound his present understanding of Christian teaching. This was an impossible programme for one book, even with frequent decisions to leave things out or acknowledgements of how much has been forgotten. Augustine begins at the beginning and scarcely gets beyond the first few verses of the first book of the Bible — which still allows him to cover an astonishing range of theological material. 'If my voice and pen confessed to you everything you explicated for me on this question, which of my readers would endure to receive it?' (*C*.12.6.6). But, if Courcelle is right about the overall purpose, the life story which most readers find so fascinating was not, from Augustine's point of view, the most important part of the *Confessions*. It was chiefly a preparation for books 11–13 — which most readers skip.

It is also, I think, unsatisfactory to treat book 10 simply as an update. If Book 10 is really a response to enquiries about what Augustine is like now, it must have disappointed the curious. He is simply not concerned to tell us how he actually spends his days as bishop of Hippo, settling lawsuits, answering letters, trying to think about his next sermon and attending endless conferences about Donatists. The one thing we learn (*C*.10.33.49–50) is that he worries about music in church — it encourages the faithful, but does it distract their fallible bishop from the content of the service? What he does, as usual, is to talk about his spiritual condition and to reflect on his own activity. But this time he does so on a larger scale, which is signalled by a kind of second preface, recalling and restating the themes of the earlier books. Whereas book 1 begins with the problem of invoking God who is beyond human knowledge, book 10 begins with a prayer to 'know as I am known'. Once again, Augustine moves between narrative and reflection on what he has been doing, and what he has been doing in books 1–9 is remembering his past in confession to God, but with a human audience, which he gradually acknowledges, also in view. So he reflects on the reasons for doing this (to arouse love for God in himself and others) and on the activity of remembering. This generates more questions about our experience of time and the oddity of presenting the eternal God with a temporally ordered account, which in turn generates questions about creation and time, and an attempt to understand the account of creation in *Genesis*. He continues to confess, but the content of his confession is now his faith, his partial understanding and the darkness that is not yet illuminated (*C*.11.2.2).

In fact, Augustine makes it quite clear (*C*.11.2.2) what he is doing. It is impossible for him to report all the promptings by which God made him a Christian; and he wants to use such time as he has to 'meditate on God's law', to acknowledge what he does and does not understand – in other words, to do theology. This is what (given the chance) he now is: a man, still subject to the distractions he has noted in book 10 (see 8), who wants to know God. 'I do not want the hours to flow away to anything else, those that I find free from the needs of restoring the body, of concentrating the mind, and of the service we owe to people or do not owe but still pay.'

Why write the 'Confessions'?

So it is misleading to think of Augustine adding books of exegesis to a work which is essentially autobiography. This is spiritual autobiography, as much concerned with his present beliefs as with his past. But the question remains: what kind of book is it, and for whom is he writing? What signals would his readers pick up, and what expectations would he raise?

We do not know why Augustine wrote the *Confessions*, or how he would have described what he was doing. It is very difficult, as successive editors and translators have found, to summarise the content of any one book of the *Confessions*, or even to provide an uncontroversial running title at the top of any one page: either you leave out something important, or you produce so detailed a paraphrase that it is hardly a summary. Similarly, the style of the *Confessions* moves in and out of different 'registers' even within a sentence: impassioned prayer, quiet narrative, Bible texts quoted and recombined and expounded, philosophical analysis of a problem, evocation of the classical canon. This is 'polyphonic discourse', not a clear melodic line.

Again, there are cross-connections with a very wide range of theological work on which Augustine was, or had been, engaged. He preached regularly on the Psalms, which were the part of Scripture he had thought about most: he had read them with great emotion after his conversion (*C*.9.4.8–11), and they were recited in the daily worship of the communities at Thagaste and Hippo. They supply much of the biblical 'inter-text' of the *Confessions*, that is, the allusions and quotations which call to mind the experience of Augustine's readers (see further 16). Augustine was also doing other work on Genesis, a text he could not leave alone. The final books of the *Confessions* are influenced by the beginnings of his theologically demanding *On the Trinity* (C.13.11.12 summarises its main theme), but he was also writing a *Literal Interpretation of Genesis*, moving between the different levels of meaning which he discusses in books 11–13 (see 11). He had been lecturing on Paul's Letter to the Romans, a text which insists that we cannot escape from sin unless God liberates us by grace, and that we may not question God's choice of those who are to be saved. Romans had transformed Augustine's own thinking on the need for God's grace and the way he interpreted his past life (see 14). His position had been clarified by questions on free will put by his old friend Simplicianus, who was now bishop of Milan, and by the continuing debate with Donatists. He had also convinced himself, in *On Christian Teaching*, that rhetoric can be used to expound Christian truth; and in the *Confessions* he uses all the rhetorical skill he can muster.

Why, then, add to all this work a book 'about me'? One answer is that reflection on his past life offered Augustine yet another mode of doing theology. In the *Confessions*, he can demonstrate the use of the Psalms, and of Scripture generally, to interpret human life. He can show how Scripture, like a human life, can be interpreted on many levels, and how wrong or inadequate interpretations of Scripture can distort a human life, as his own had been distorted by the crude readings and rejections taught him by the Manichees. It is a principle of interpretation for him that not only words, but events, can be a 'figure' for other events, just as many episodes in the Old Testament were taken to prefigure events of the New Testament. So one man's life, described with exceptional vividness, can – to change the metaphor – be a microcosm, a small-scale example of alienation from God and redemption by God's active love; just as, in the Platonist philosophical tradition, the workings of one man's mind and memory can help us rise to an understanding of the nature of God. And one book can move from a narrative of one man's relationship with God to reflection on God's action in time and human understanding of God's work.

Another answer is that the *Confessions* is overdetermined — there were simply too many reasons for writing it. Augustine was in his first few years as a bishop, and was very much a public figure. He had to come to terms with the expectation that he, a sinner in need of help, could bring God's word to his people; and he was living with his African past. So the *Confessions* was an act of therapy. But he also needed to explain his past, especially the time he had spent away from Africa, to others. Hostile critics had spread rumours about his Manichee connection, and doubts about his conversion, which he wanted to refute. Friends and admirers wanted to know how the successful rhetorician had returned to God, his homeland and an ascetic lifestyle; their admiration was itself a danger, distracting them from awareness that Augustine, like them, was a person trying to live as God wants. Augustine wanted to give people a proper understanding of God's work in creation and redemption, and warn them off destructive errors which he knew only too well. One simple answer to the question 'What kind of book is this?' is 'It is a book about Augustine and what matters to him.' So perhaps we should rephrase the question and ask instead 'What did Augustine, and Augustine's readers, think important in a life?'

8 'I want to know all about you'

This prompts another question: who were the expected readers of the *Confessions*? It is an intellectually demanding book, and it assumes both a shared cultural background of literature and philosophy (see 16) and a commitment to, or at least a strong interest in, Christianity. We might wonder whether Augustine envisaged many such readers in the African church or on its fringes, apart from the circle of friends who had shared his life at Thagaste. But there is reason to think that he expected a wider circulation for the *Confessions*.

Paulinus and the ascetic connection

A year or so before Augustine started work on the *Confessions*, in summer 395, his close friend Alypius (who like him became a bishop, of their home town Thagaste) wrote to Paulinus of Nola. Paulinus was a spectacular example of renouncing the world: he was a Spanish landowner, related to half the Roman aristocracy (including Ambrose), who had sold most of his estates, given the proceeds to the poor, and retired to live chastely with his wife as priest of a shrine at Nola in southern Italy. Here he received pilgrims and corresponded with other ascetic Christians in a wonderful amalgam of late antique politeness and Christian self-deprecation, of the culture they shared as Romans and the Bible they shared as Christians. (In case this sounds very depressing, he also had a sense of humour: witness his elaborate thanks for the gift of a camel-hair cloak, as worn by John the Baptist. How many improving thoughts, he exclaims, will be inspired by its profitable bristles and salutary itch! His return gift – hopelessly inferior, of course – is a lambswool tunic.) Paulinus had been an example to inspire Augustine and Alypius, and Alypius decided to make contact, sending Paulinus some anti-Manichaean works of Augustine – perhaps he hoped to counter any damaging rumours – and asking for the *Chronicle* of the church historian Eusebius. Paulinus sent a copy, with a personal request.

I particularly ask this of you: since you have embraced me, undeserving as I am, in your great love, that in return for this history of events you send me the whole history of Your Sanctity, so as to declare 'of what race, from what homeland you come' called by so great a master, and from what causes 'separated from your mother's womb' you passed over to the mother of the sons of God who rejoices in her offspring, and joined 'a royal and a priestly people'. As you have mentioned that you learned the name of my lowliness at Milan, I admit to a special eagerness to learn – so that I may know you in all respects and be able to congratulate you the more – whether Ambrose, my father in that he took me up, invited you to faith or consecrated you priest, so that we both owe our being to the same man.

(Paulinus, *Letter* 3.4)

Paulinus, like Augustine in the *Confessions*, moves freely in and out of the two main intertexts of the cultivated western Christian in the late fourth century. The first of his quotations is from the *Aeneid*, the second and third are from the New Testament. 'Your Sanctity' and 'my lowliness' are Christian adaptations of a useful late antique convention in which the titles used express the approach of the person writing and what he hopes is true of the person addressed. (An emperor, for instance, might have written to a civil servant 'Our Benevolence sincerely hopes that Your Efficiency will soon be able to locate that file on tax concessions for teachers of rhetoric.') Both the style and the conscious modesty create expectations for the tone of Alypius' reply.

Alypius and Monica: small-scale biography

Alypius was eager to establish a link with Paulinus, but he was too modest altogether to write about himself; so Augustine took over, just as (we learn from the *Confessions*) he had taken the lead in so much of Alypius' life.

Soon, with God's help, I shall put all of Alypius in your heart. What really worries me is that he would be afraid to reveal everything the Lord has done for him, in case a less intelligent reader – for such things would not be read by you alone – should take it not as God's gifts to humankind, but Alypius boasting about himself.

(*Letter* 27.5)

Augustine likewise offers all of himself to Paulinus, as Paulinus in his letter has offered himself to them. Is the *Confessions* a response to Paulinus' welcoming this offer? It seems, at the very least, likely that this exchange of letters is one of the triggers for the *Confessions*, and that the account of Alypius in *Confessions* 6 is very much what Augustine wrote for Paulinus.

'I want to know all about you', in this context, has a quite specific content. Where are you from? How did you come to be a Christian priest or ascetic? Are you one of Ambrose's too? These are the familiar moves of people in the same profession establishing links. The questions do not ask for a narrative of personal history up to this point, but for the aspects of one person's life which confirm and encourage others who are trying to do the same in theirs. Paulinus, in the letter quoted above, dismisses the time before he was a Christian: Ambrose was the father who lifted the reborn Paulinus in his arms. In this context, the emphasis is not on personal achievement, but on what God has done for this person; and it can be assumed that the account is not marked 'private and confidential', but will be passed on to other readers with similar interests and connections. Fourth-century ascetics, in fact, were much given to networking: it was not only the most efficient method of getting books, but also a way of keeping in touch with spiritual developments.

The account of Alypius, in *Confessions* 6, is shaped by these expectations. We are told, briefly, that Alypius was from the same home town as Augustine, from a leading municipal family; he was Augustine's student at Thagaste and Carthage, studying rhetoric as a necessary part of law. What follows is concerned with Alypius' progress (very much under the influence of Augustine) to Christian commitment. His addiction to 'the games' (see 5), which can be overcome only by God, is balanced by a story of his wrongful arrest at Carthage, which taught him not to be hasty in condemning the apparently guilty, and by praise of his integrity as a lawyer. He resisted bribery and intimidation; and also a temptation, which Augustine must have understood only too well, to get books he wanted for himself copied, free of charge, by the government staff he could use for official documents. Alypius' theological progress is linked with Augustine's, but described in far less detail: Augustine does not linger on the damage he must have done to Alypius and other admirers who followed him into Manichaeism. Alypius took longer than Augustine to admit Christ into his Platonism (*C*.9.4.7), was baptised with Augustine (*C*.9.6.14) – and there the story ends.

The account of Monica (*C*.9.8.17–13.37) is similar in kind. Perhaps, again, Augustine was reusing material he had written, something to replace the funeral laudation he might have given had she died in Africa. Monica is constantly praised for her profound Christian confidence and her devotion to the son whose defection hurts her so badly. (Post-Freudian readers – see 10 – find this a damaging kind of motherhood, but Augustine's readers would have agreed with Ambrose, *C*.6.2.2, in telling him how lucky he was.) But Monica too has weaknesses. As a child, strictly brought up, she almost becomes addicted to wine: the ancient world saw this as one of the greatest dangers for women, since it weakened their chastity. She escapes the danger because one of the slaves shames her out of it. In Italy, she has to shed some mistaken traditions of African Christianity, though she does this willingly when instructed by Ambrose (*C*.6.1.1–2.2).

Above all, Monica has to abandon the worldly hopes for her son which had dictated too many of her responses to his conduct. She was probably to blame for not seeing him safely married (*C*.2.2.3, 2.2.8) once sexual desire began to trouble him: no doubt she was looking higher than a respectable girl from the provinces. Augustine uses Virgil to suggest to us that her feelings when he left Carthage for Italy were not wholly admirable. In the hope of avoiding a scene, he set sail when she was not expecting it, having falsely told her that he was seeing off a friend: he leaves her lamenting (*C*.5.8.15) on the shore at Carthage. When Aeneas similarly slipped away from Carthage, leaving Dido frantic with grief and frustrated love, he was obeying the gods and carrying out his mission to found Rome. Dido was – however understandably – in the wrong, a woman in whom passion had displaced awareness of her own duty to her people and of the overall plan of the gods. Monica's grief is presented as loss combined with anxiety that her son was taking the wrong path, but its intensity suggests that she was allowing feeling to displace faith. She follows Augustine to Italy and arranges a marriage (*C*.6.13.23) which will further his career. He has to send away the woman he has lived with since his student days, and replaces her (*C*.6.15.25) with a temporary sexual partner: once again, though he does not say so, his mother's worldly good sense has made him fall into sin. It is Augustine's conversion, his decision to live in chastity and abandon his career, which also liberates Monica from her worldly ambitions for him.

The closure of Monica's story is imposed by her death, but the stories of Augustine and Alypius are closed at that same point, while they wait for a passage home to Africa to lead a life in God's service. The *Confessions* tells us nothing of their life as members of a pioneering monastic community back at Thagaste, or as priest and bishop: instead, Augustine talks entirely in terms of spiritual problems and God's help. Images of past sexual activity (*C*.10.30.41), hunger which needs to be satisfied without excess (*C*.10.31.43−7), praise from admirers (*C*.10.37.60−2), are all hazards which he needs help to negotiate. As others have remarked, you would never know, from the *Confessions*, that the author is the overworked bishop of a minority church in a situation much like that of Northern Ireland (see 6). Augustine's past did not include Donatism, so he does not deal with the hazards of Donatist theology. But the kind of life story which would interest Paulinus also had its uses in Augustine's immediate situation. In the *Confessions*, the Donatist claim to be the true church in Africa, the 'gathered church' of the righteous, is tacitly challenged by his insistence that human beings are not righteous, but are slaves of sin freed only by the action of God. This is true of Alypius, of Monica, and above all of Augustine himself: all have failings and all need God's help throughout their lives.

9 Spiritual biography

The autobiography of the *Confessions*, then, has a particular focus. Past life (and present lifestyle) is important only in so far as it displays God's mercy and explains the spiritual state of the person who is now struggling to live a God-centred life. In this respect, there are precedents and parallels for the *Confessions*. Some Christians, in the time before Christianity was an acceptable religion, told the story of how they came to a faith which put them at risk, as in the second-century 'con-version narratives' by Justin Martyr and by Cyprian of Carthage (both men with a rhetorical and philosophical training). After

Constantine's profession of Christianity, as martyrdom came to be replaced by the 'long martyrdom' of ascetic life, a literature of renunciation and spiritual struggle developed. Athanasius' *Life of Antony* (a Latin translation by Evagrius was available from c. 370) inspired many others besides the secret policemen at Trier (*C*.8.6.15). There were brief histories of some Desert Fathers included in the collections of their sayings. There was a reverent biography of Melania, a Roman heiress whose estate at Thagaste, only one among her multi-national holdings, was considerably bigger than the town. Jerome, writing letters obviously designed for public reading, describes his own experience of asceticism and the merits of the great Roman ladies who also abandoned their wealth. We can see how the information Augustine gives in the *Confessions*, handled by an admiring outsider, could turn into hagiography – and in a biography by the devoted Possidius, a member of his community at Hippo, he does indeed become a paragon. It is no wonder that Alypius lost his nerve, or that Augustine refused to end the *Confessions* at book 9 as if, once converted, he had achieved instant sanctity and lived happily ever after. But, by addressing God in praise and admission of weakness, Augustine avoids the risk (for him, not just a social but a spiritual danger) of exhibiting pride and self-reliance.

Christians who seemed to others to be spiritual heroes were themselves overwhelmingly aware of weakness and danger. In the later fourth century, Christian ascetics were developing a remarkable collective experience of self-examination, some of which was recorded (by Evagrius in the east and John Cassian in the west) in classic guides to the spiritual life. Living in solitude or in communities organised for prayer, work and Bible study, seeking advice from those spiritually more advanced, these people became intensely conscious of the desires and failings which separated them from God. They felt themselves to be under attack by the forces of evil which could exploit the weaknesses of a human heart not yet committed wholly to God, and they did not dare to suppose that they would not succumb: they told the story of the monk who, after years of lonely struggle against lust, was found racing off to town in search of a prostitute.

This is very much the tone of the *Confessions*. Antony, so Athanasius says, advised monks to write down their actions and the promptings of their heart, as if for others to read: the fear of being found out would help them, even if their confession remained secret. Augustine's motivation is different: he knows he has readers, and hopes to encourage them if they think it is all too difficult and themselves too weak − of course they are, but help is at hand as it is for him (*C*.10.3.4). The predominant tone, the emphasis on weakness and uncertainty and the ever-present risk of sin, belongs not just to Christian late antiquity, but to one particular strand within it − some would say to Augustine himself. Many people in Augustine's own lifetime, notably the British ascetic Pelagius and the southern French monastics, thought he overdid the uncertainty: baptised Christians could be sure that God would not let them go. But if the tone is new, the literary form is not. Examining one's own conduct and motives, for the benefit of a reader or a student, is a very ancient technique: perhaps even the oldest form of anything we would recognise as biography.

Biography and autobiography

Writings which focus on an individual life − the record of a king's achievements, or a poet rejoicing or bewailing his fate − go back long before Herodotus established the principles of history-writing in the mid-fifth century BC. But few people would accept that this is biography, the description of a complete life, and many have argued that biography really began in fourth-century BC Greece, with the life of Socrates expounded by his students and defenders. The Greek word *bios* means both the life of an individual and the lifestyle he (almost without exception 'he') followed. Biography was often concerned with philosophers, whose way of living was an expression of their principles and so of legitimate interest to their students. There were occasional 'debunking' biographies (of Pythagoras, for instance), but the usual reason for writing the life of a philosopher, especially in late antiquity, was to show how he had achieved nearness to the gods by his super-human self-control and intellectual ability, and to inspire his students to follow his example.

The emphasis of biography was on the mature achievement which had made the subject worthy of having a biography written about him. Anecdotes of childhood and youth were included only if they foreshadowed future greatness. (This trend continued into fourth-century Christian biography: we hear about the boy Athanasius playing baptisms with his friends, and the boy Ambrose, seeing his female relatives kiss a bishop's hand, extending his own hand to be kissed.) Thus the lives of 'great men', that is national leaders, were mostly conveyed in the history of their times, with the occasional minor anecdote or item of personal information to make their presence and personality more vivid (something like the famous footnotes in A.J.P. Taylor's *Britain 1914—45*, of which the most notorious is on George V: 'his trousers were creased at the sides, not at the back and front'). Biographers varied in the amount of personal detail they gave — or were able to discover. Suetonius, who researched in the imperial archives early in the second century, is able to provide in *The Twelve Caesars* all kinds of fascinating information on the health, habits and dinner-party conversation of Roman emperors. (Augustus wore four tunics in winter, and woollen underwear.) He gives the impression of narrating historical events only as a background for his portrait of a remarkable human being. Plutarch, writing about the same time, thought (*Life of Alexander* 1.1—2) that a passing remark may tell a biographer far more about his subject than a battle in which thousands died. He distinguishes biography from history in that biography recounts actions to illustrate individual character, not as a complete historical record, but his *Lives* are essentially history with the focus on an individual.

Twentieth-century readers are usually surprised by the way in which character is presented in these biographies. There is very little sense of a person growing, developing, shaped by seemingly trivial experience or by motivations which remain obscure. Birth, upbringing and temperament may be noted, but there is no evocation of a physical and social setting, the 'feel' of a particular time and place and family. It is a large, but I think a correct, generalisation that childhood was found interesting chiefly in terms of education (which is not to say that parents in the ancient world were indifferent to their children: some were obviously besotted); so the actions of the adult tend not to be explained by the experience of the child, except in the most general terms. Motivation may be debated — was this politician a genuine reformer or just ambitious? why exactly did he make this move? — but it is simple and recognisable, and action 'out of character' either reveals the true nature which had been concealed, or is flatly recorded as extraordinary. Plutarch notes, for instance, that the politician Crassus (rival of Julius Caesar), a notoriously shrewd and cautious financier and an experienced soldier, was absurdly reckless in pursuit of military glory at the end of his life; and comments that it is very puzzling. Adult character is assumed to be stable, the result of individual temperament and of habituation.

Autobiographies, in so far as they survive, revealed little more. Great men wrote about their own achievements: autobiography linked itself to history, presenting one man's version of events, supposedly without fear or favour but usually to his advantage and certainly not to his disadvantage. (The elder Cato, in the second century BC, wrote *On His Own Virtues*.) There was neither a distinctive name for autobiography (nor was there until early in the nineteenth century), nor a distinctive set of expectations. The detail of daily life and relationships, or of personal feeling, belonged to other literary forms. Two (very different) examples known to Augustine are the *Epistles* of Horace, relatively short hexameter poems in which simple moral messages are conveyed through narrative or discursive comment, and the *Golden Ass* of Apuleius, a novel about the adventures of one Lucius after he is turned into a donkey. It so happens that Apuleius (a second-century AD writer) came from Madaura, where Augustine was at school; he was a Platonist philosopher as well as a novelist, and the *Golden Ass* (otherwise known as the *Metamorphoses*) can be read as an allegory of a soul lost through addiction to sexual pleasure and misguided curiosity, and redeemed by the direct intervention of the goddess Isis. Both the *Epistles* and the *Metamorphoses* connect with a long philosophical tradition of reflecting on one's daily life with the aim of moral improvement, removing errors and muddles and practising good conduct, and this is where we find the detail of personal life and motivation, described by the person who knows most about them.

Self-examination

Philosophers from Socrates on had encouraged their students to think about what they were doing, what motives and desires they were hiding from themselves, and whether their life was rightly directed. (Aristotle, for instance, remarked that those who seek high status are really trying to convince themselves that they are worth something.) There was always the possibility that a philosopher would decide his life needed radical change: 'conversion' is not peculiar to Christianity or to late antiquity. Stoic philosophers, in particular, were taught to deal with the crises of life by assessing their responses and deciding whether these were in accord with their principles. The first-century philosopher Epictetus offers an example: imagine yourself waiting to see the emperor, who may order you killed or send you to a prison island. Are you frightened? That is because you think he can harm you. But you know, from rigorous argument, that your true self cannot be harmed by anything which happens to you − only by the way you react, which is within your power. So the emperor cannot harm you and fear is an inappropriate response. Dismiss it.

Seneca, a contemporary of Epictetus, wrote *Moral Letters* in this tradition, using his own behaviour and reactions as a way of teaching his addressee. The *Letters* do not provide a history of his life, but they do describe episodes and encounters which offer a moral lesson: for instance, Seneca makes unkind remarks about the decrepit old slave on the door, only to find that the man is his contemporary. Seneca was tutor and then minister to the emperor Nero, but his writings declared that what is really important in a life is not political but moral achievement. The great question is whether, in high office or in cultivated retirement or in exile, you succeed in living in accordance with your principles. For Seneca, a Stoic, this meant aligning your own will with the purposes of divine providence.

The most famous work in this tradition was written by a man who held the highest possible office, the emperor Marcus Aurelius, in the mid-second century. It is known as the *Meditations*, but its title is *To Himself*. Its form is that of a private notebook of self-exhortation and moral comment, some of it written in his tent at the end of a hard day's campaign against the Dacians, when he lacks the philosophical books and companionship which would usually keep him on the right lines. Marcus, like Augustine, noted events and people who had made him what he was, and was grateful for the guidance of the gods which, as he could see when he looked back, had saved him from error. But his book belongs to a different moral universe from Augustine's. Here, for instance, is part of his first section, a short retrospect of his life and what he owes to different people and to the gods.

From the gods: good grandparents, good parents, a good sister, good teachers, relatives and friends good almost without exception. And that I did not fall into causing offence to any of them, even though I had a temperament which might have made me do so if the occasion had arisen. It was the kindness of the gods that there occurred no conjunction of events which would put me to the proof. And that I was not brought up for any longer time by my grandfather's mistress, and that I did not become a man before due season, but even delayed a little ... That I had such a brother, who was able by his character to rouse me to take care of myself, and at the same time encouraged me with respect and affection. That my children were neither mentally defective nor deformed in body. That I progressed no further in rhetoric, composition and the other arts in which I should perhaps have been absorbed, had I seen myself making easy progress.   (1.17)

Marcus is aware of his own temperament and his intellectual limitations, of the benefits he has received from the gods and the hazards they have helped him to avoid. He does not agonise as Augustine does about the experience of sexual desire, or imperfect relationships, or the use of language to convey fiction, as manifestations of human sin and alienation from God; he is grateful to the gods for what they have given him, without considering himself unworthy and corrupt. In rather the same spirit, W. H. Auden once preached on Jesus' story of the Pharisee and the tax-collector (Luke 18.9—14), arguing that the Pharisee was quite right to thank God for the benefits of his upbringing and character, which made it easy for him to avoid some kinds of sin: where he went wrong was in saying 'Lord, I thank Thee that I am not as other men, extortioners, unjust, adulterers, or even as this tax-collector', because of course he was, like them, liable to sin. By these standards, Marcus is simply trying to assess himself correctly and to be thankful that there are some problems he does not have.

What are people like?

The common assumption of this philosophical tradition is that we can analyse our motives and conduct, and, when shown our absurdity, behave better by deciding to do so and by establishing better habits. Aristotle, in a famous discussion of why people do things they know to be wrong, concluded that either they do not really know it to be wrong − they are simply parroting what they have been told − or they do know it but have temporarily lost sight of their knowledge under the influence of desire, or drink, or madness. It does not make sense to suppose that, if I really and at this moment know that (say) murder is wrong and therefore destructive to me as well as my victim, I shall go ahead and do it. Many people in the fourth century shared such beliefs, including the more confident kind of Christian. But Christian ascetic tradition had far less confidence in the power of reason and good habits; and whereas the common experience of Graeco-Roman philosophers was that the practice of philosophy brought them closer to God, the common experience of Christian religious was (and is) that those who, to outsiders, seem closest to God are most acutely conscious of what separates people from God.

Hence the anguish over aspects of human life which others take for granted, and the willingness to describe oneself as a sinful failure.

Many philosophers have thought that true human nature, uncorrupted by social pressures, appears in the human infant. The late twentieth-century western version of this 'cradle argument' is that the uncorrupted child eagerly explores her environment and responds to love. Augustine sees in human fancy both God's goodness, which ensures that the mother is glad to respond to the needs of her child, and the beginnings of human alienation from God in greed and jealousy. Readers often feel that he overdoes the guilt: what is so bad about a baby who does not want another to be fed first (*C*.1.7.11), or a gang of teenagers (*C*.2.4.9, 2.6.12) scrumping pears? As mothers and nurses told Augustine, 'Oh, he'll grow out of it.' But why was he like that in the first place? What has happened to human beings that a baby should grudge milk to his brother, who like himself would die without it, when there is plenty for both? Why should it be pleasurable to steal something you neither need nor even enjoy? 'Is *that* the innocence of childhood?' (*C*.1.19.30).

When people say the *Confessions* is the first autobiography, that is because they expect an autobiography to be a life-history which reveals the inner feelings and self-awareness of the writer. Augustine's account of his life is not a wholly new form, but (at least in part) a transposition of the tradition of self-analysis. It depends on the assumption that what matters in a life, and therefore in the description of a life, is the attainment of goodness, but it rejects the assumption that an exact moral analysis is most of the battle. Augustine frequently describes an experience or a state of mind, and then 'freezes' his narrative while he discusses what exactly is happening. Even in the highly charged account of his conversion to a life of chastity, he stops (*C*.8.9.21–10.24) to engage in careful and lucid discussion of a philosophical problem: what exactly is happening when I make an act of will but do not carry it out? Who or what is giving the instruction and resisting it? Are there actually two or more wills at work when there are conflicting choices to be made? It is very important here to reach the right conclusion: there is not some alien force at work which is 'not me' and which can be discarded, but there is one person trying to reach a decision. In the philosophical tradition (and in some people's experience) it is enough to state the problem correctly. Augustine − having demonstrated that he can do so with great efficiency − insists that his own experience shows it is not enough. God has to intervene, and only then does it become possible to act and to understand what the direction of life has really been. But if clarity is not enough, how can Augustine select and convey to his readers the true direction and the misdirections of his life?

Chapter 3

True Confessions? Narrative and memory

10 What really happened?

How do they know, when they hear from me about me, whether I am telling the truth, since no one knows what is going on in a human being except the spirit of the human being, which is in him?
(*C*.10.3.3)

But how does even the human spirit know what is going on, unless God tells it the truth (*C*.10.5.7)? Is there a definitive account of a human life, and can it be given during that lifetime by the person who is living the life, or by anyone else? Augustine reiterates, at critical moments in his story, that he could not see where he was going, or why, or what was really important − like Robert Graves's butterfly who 'lurches here and there by guess and God and hope and hopelessness'. He also acknowledges that there are many things he has forgotten, or that he misunderstood at the time. In book 10 he breaks any dramatic illusion by making us look at the man who has told us the story and who is still wrestling with temptation and confusion. He describes (*C*.10.8.12) the experience of searching his memory and finding that what comes to mind is not what he wanted. So how can we believe his present confession?

Some of Augustine's first readers were prepared to accuse him of deliberate lies, or at least of misrepresentation. The senior bishop of Numidia had expressed some (quite reasonable) anxieties about his ordination as bishop, after so little experience of the church, especially when nothing was known about his baptism at Milan and rather too much was remembered about his youth. His Donatist enemies, and his former Manichee friends, seized on this. A Manichee, Secundinus, accused him of leaving the sect only from fear of persecution, not because their teachings had been refuted. A Donatist, Petilianus, said he was still a crypto-Manichee and further up the hierarchy than a simple Hearer; he had left Carthage because the governor expelled him (but this was wrong on dates, as Augustine could show); and he was still at heart a rhetorician and an adept of dialectic, given over to pagan culture. Augustine had to defend himself at the Carthage council of 403; when he says (C.10.3.3) that his fellow-Christians will, in charity, believe him, these accusations are the background. One message of book 10 is 'This is what I am now, not a Manichee, but a Christian seeking truth.'

Twentieth-century critics have been more concerned with Augustine's very rapid progress (see 5) from Platonism to Christianity. Is he trying to maximise his connection with Ambrose and minimise his connection with the Milan Platonists? Why does he say so little, in books 7–9, about the Catholic faith, and was his conversion really to Platonism? But they have also put forward a more radical challenge. Augustine may be trying to tell the truth, but suppose he has got it all wrong? From his perspective in the late fourth century, the guiding theme is God's intervention, often undetected at the time, to rescue a human soul from falsehood, error and the habit of sin. But some twentieth-century readers think there is a different underlying story: Augustine is really describing, with unprecedented clarity, the problems which most interested Freud in human life, that is his relationship with his parents and his attitude to sexuality.

Freud and Augustine

Augustine's father Patricius is not much in evidence in the *Confessions* – nor, indeed, is any member of Augustine's family except his mother. Patricius is presented as a passionate man who disregards Christian teaching until his deathbed, and who rejoices when he notices (C.2.3.6), at the baths, that his son is becoming capable of begetting sons. Augustine's mother, on the contrary, tries to deny her son's sexuality, and, as Augustine himself puts it, to replace his earthly father by a father in heaven (C.1.11.17). Patricius dies just as Augustine himself embarks on adolescent rule-breaking and sexual turmoil: his death is reported later, in parenthesis (*C*.3.4.7), with what psychologists know as lack of affect.

It is an odd and interesting parenthesis. Augustine is describing how he reached Cicero's *Hortensius* in the standard curriculum at Carthage, and found it had transformed his ambitions.

Suddenly, all empty hope was cheapened, and I desired the immortality of wisdom with an incredible ardour in my heart, and I began to rise up to return to you. So it was not to the sharpening of my tongue, which is what I seemed to be buying at my mother's expense − I was nineteen and my father had died two years earlier − it was not, then, to the sharpening of my tongue that I applied the book, nor did it impress upon me its style, but what it was saying.

In the parable of the Prodigal Son which Jesus told, the son who has left home and squandered his inheritance is reduced to being a swineherd and eating pigswill; at last he decides to 'rise up and return to my father' (Luke 15.18), that is, to go back to God. Augustine's earthly father is dismissed both as a spiritual and as a practical force in his life.

The death of a friend (*C*.4.7.12), by contrast, makes his home town intolerable. Augustine is never alone in the *Confessions*, but (even when we know from other texts that family members were with him) the relationships he describes are those established by the shared pursuit of knowledge. In his dialogue *The Teacher*, his son Adeodatus becomes his − very bright − student. The death of Adeodatus (*C*.9.6.14) is also noted out of sequence, though Augustine here explains his lack of anxiety as the effect of faith. In the *Confessions* Augustine takes the lead, never finding a tutor or father-figure of his own. Faustus the Manichee is charming but not clever enough, Ambrose is obviously too busy − and perhaps, if they had ever had time to talk, Augustine would have found that he was cleverer even than Ambrose. It seems that Augustine can cope with the teacher-student relationship, but not with being a father or a son.

This − you might think − is wilful misunderstanding. In a book concerned with Augustine's spiritual and intellectual development, the people who influenced him in discussion must be important. Teachers and students are bound to matter in the life of an academic. Most young people mind more intensely about their friends, who have chosen them, than about their parents, and for Augustine the non-possessive love of friends is theologically as well as personally vital (*C*.6.16.26). But perhaps this is only a defensive reaction: the Freudian case can be made stronger.

When Augustine goes home to teach after his time at Carthage, his mother, who now controls the family money, throws him out of the house because he is a Manichee. Reassured by a vision (*C*.3.11.19) in which he is standing beside her on a ruler — which she interprets to mean that he abides by the rule — she tries to keep him near her in Africa. 'The son of all these tears cannot be lost', said a sensible bishop who refused to argue with Augustine about Manichaeism (*C*.3.12.21), and it is tempting to translate this as a recognition of emotional blackmail. When Augustine leaves Monica (not daring to tell her he is doing so, and invoking in his narrative Aeneas leaving Dido to suicide, *C*.5.8.15), she recovers from despair and follows him to Italy, where she succeeds in displacing his long-term lover with a child-fiancée who is too young to marry. Her triumph comes when he abandons both the career and the sexuality which took him from her, and prepares for their return home together. Christian readers in the early centuries AD enjoyed variants on the standard plot of the ancient novel, in which a pair of lovers are separated, tested and finally reunited: here is the filial romance. Monica and Augustine are united (*C*.9.10.23) in a shared vision. Now she can die in peace, and Augustine, who mentioned his father's death in parenthesis and his son's in a sentence or two, describes with intense and lengthy recall his reaction to her death (*C*.9.12.29–31). He is left obsessed with sexuality as the manifestation of human sin, and with the need for reconciliation through knowledge with a father-God. But he cannot understand this father's purposes, and the only response to his pleas and questions is in the words of a text which he must correctly interpret or perish; just as the worldly future of the child Augustine once depended on understanding Virgil, who supplied him with images of destructive love and of journeys in obedience to a stern father.

Such a reading cannot be refuted, but will not satisfy any reader who thinks that God is more than a projection of psychic impulses. Late Roman culture offers plenty of ammunition for Freudians. Sons, even adult sons, were expected to obey their fathers. The father's authority to instruct and punish, as head of household, is one of Augustine's dominant images for the ordering of society. The child's entry into human society, he observes in *Confessions* 1, is marked by coercion: the baby cries, the schoolchild is beaten. Augustine swings between a characteristic conviction that it was all his fault and the child's resentment of false adult values. 'The amusement of adults is called business' (*C*.1.9.15); grown-ups spend hours at the games and punish their children for neglecting school-work; they refuse to take seriously beatings which are a real terror to their children; and whatever they say, they mind more about manners and worldly success (*C*.3.3.5) than about morals. Augustine reflects in book 10 on the oddity of remembering emotion without feeling it, but in the books about his childhood (as often in autobiography) emotion is very strong.

Augustine and sexuality

Sons were also expected to defer to the wishes of mothers. The tradition of Roman motherhood was to show commitment to your children by strong moral concern and by fairmindedness in assigning your property, and also by urging your son to the achievements which society denied to you. Personal nurture in childhood, encouragement of the child's interests, leaving him space to grow in the confidence that you accept him for what he is – all this is a very recent ideal for the middle-class mother. So is the ideal of marriage as a strong emotional commitment chosen by the parties. In Roman society, marriage was (by definition) a relationship for the procreation of legitimate children, and was usually negotiated by families. Affection and respect were likely to develop if both parties behaved well; but in a society which had no welfare net, the emphasis was on children's deference to the reasonable wishes of the parents who invested money and effort in them, not on love and self-determination.

Twentieth-century readers almost always condemn Augustine for sending away his concubine so that his mother could negotiate a marriage to someone still a child. It was a long-standing and sexually fulfilling relationship (*C*.4.2.2, 6.15.25); they had a son; he was deeply wounded by losing her; he never even tells us her name. How could he? But, by fourth-century standards, what else could he do? It was quite usual to arrange a betrothal before the girl (and sometimes the boy) was ready for marriage. The legal age of marriage, for a girl, was twelve, and it was assumed that she was then biologically mature. It was also usual for a man to delay marriage until he was established in a career, and far more respectable for him to have a live-in partner than to resort to prostitutes or (much worse) pursue other men's wives or daughters.

I use the Roman technical term 'concubine', which means a woman who is not married but is the acknowledged partner of one man, because 'mistress' or 'lover' or 'girlfriend' imports the wrong assumptions. Men had, as a rule, good reason for not marrying their concubines. Sometimes the woman could not make a legal marriage, because she was a slave, or had started out as an actress or an entertainer; but even if she could, she was almost certain to belong to the lower classes in a society which formalised class distinction in law. (The 'lower orders', *humiliores*, could even be tortured to give evidence and suffered physical punishments which the 'more respectable', *honestiores*, were spared.) Marriage to the concubine would have meant the abandonment of all Augustine had worked for and Monica had financed, and he could not have continued the relationship once his marriage was arranged. It was taken for granted that men had casual sexual relationships with lower-class women or slaves, but a permanent commitment was an insult to the lawful wife, and the family of Augustine's future bride would never have tolerated it.

Augustine's concubine was leading the best life she could by her fidelity to him and her decision to live in chastity after they parted: it is a sign of respect, not of neglect, that he does not publicise her name. When he wrote *On the Good of Marriage*, he said that a man who dismisses a faithful concubine to marry another woman has committed what Jesus called 'adultery in the heart' – and the adultery is against the concubine, not the intended wife. Not all Christians shared this opinion. Bishop Leo of Rome, in the mid-fifth century, authorised Christian men to dismiss a concubine and marry, on the grounds that this was not bigamy, but moral improvement. Augustine is not complacent about his own conduct: he knew it was not to his credit (*C*.6.12.22) that he was held by a sexual bond instead of a commitment to raise children.

Augustine's views on sexuality are rooted in late Roman culture. It was a philosophical commonplace, dating back to Plato, that sexual activity binds humans to the body and diverts energy from the exercise of reason. Augustine was not alone in pointing out that sexual response, or its absence, defies rational control. But many of his fellow-Christians thought that, in his later theology, he overemphasised sexual guilt as he did moral helplessness. Like their non-Christian contemporaries, they thought that sexual desire had its God-given use in the procreation of children within marriage. They were not prepared to think, as Augustine eventually did, that children are born infected with the lust which was biologically necessary for their conception – even though this 'original sin' is a tidy explanation for the greed and possessiveness which worried Augustine in little children. Augustine had to defend himself against the charge (derived in part from the *Confessions*) that he was still Manichaean in his suspicion of sex, just as now he needs defending against the charge that his theology, indeed his Christian commitment, is the result of a childhood he was not equipped to understand.

11 Multiple readings and exegesis

We can guess what Augustine would have replied to this charge: how do others know what was actually happening in his life? But he would have to admit that all he can offer is a reading of God's purposes. He confesses to God and appeals to God for enlightenment: the *Confessions* is not a soliloquy addressed to himself, but extended prayer addressed to God. God does not speak in this long conversation, except in the verses of Scripture which come to Augustine's mind, in the biblical intertext of his life. God has written a book, and Augustine is happy with books. But a dominant theme of the *Confessions*, exemplified in the last three books, is that Scripture can be read in many ways and understood at different levels (*C*.6.5.8). ' "It means what I say." "No, it means what I say." I think there is more true piety in saying "Why not both, if both are true, or a third or a fourth interpretation or whatever other truth anyone has ever found in these words?" ' (*C*.12.31.42).

The techniques of exegesis which Augustine learnt from Ambrose's preaching can be used on his own work. Augustine envisaged God not so much dictating the Bible as commissioning authors for its various books: he once, perhaps wistfully, speculates 'If I had then been what Moses was, and You had assigned me the book of Genesis to write ...' (*C*.12.26.36). A particular author's choice and ordering of words repay study, just as in school readings of Virgil or modern 'close readings'. Scripture has its own usages which are not necessarily those of ordinary speech. But the Bible is what is now called a megatext − a corpus of texts which must be studied together − and verses should be interpreted not in isolation, but in context, which means the full range of biblical teaching even if it could not have been known to the relevant author. Thus Augustine, seeking to understand (*C*.13.6.7−7.8) why the Spirit was 'borne above the waters' in Genesis 1.2, invokes phrases of Paul on the supereminent love of the Spirit which lifts us above the waters of the material world. If there are apparent contradictions in Scripture, they can be resolved by attention to different levels of meaning. For instance, in his *On the Trinity*, Augustine rescues Paul from a charge of directly contradicting Genesis. Paul says (I Corinthians 11.7) that man is in the image of God, but woman is the image and glory of man, whereas Genesis says God created humanity in God's own image: male and female God created them. Augustine concludes that Paul has in mind the physical inferiority (which seemed to him an obvious fact) of woman, whereas Genesis refers to the spiritual equality of male and female. (The point recurs in *C.*13.32.47, where the physical subordination of female to male is seen as analogous with the subordination of desire to guiding reason.) Augustine summarised the principles of exegesis in *On Christian Teaching*: any verse of the Bible which is not obviously teaching either good conduct or Christian faith should be interpreted allegorically.

Such techniques were not peculiarly Christian devices for 'saving the text', but were common to late antiquity. They were used also in Jewish interpretation of Torah and in the attempts of Platonist philosophers to reconcile not just Plato and Aristotle, but the traditions of mythology which Plato had condemned. (Thus the horrific story of the god Kronos who swallows his children becomes an allegory of time, *chronos* in Greek, absorbing what it produces so that the present is always becoming the past − a problem which interests Augustine in book 11. Alternatively, the name Kronos is interpreted as a combination of the Greek word *koros*, satiety, with *nous*, mind, and the Latin equivalent Saturnus as a combination of Latin *satur*, satiated, with Greek *nous*, so that Kronos/Saturn, father of the supreme god Zeus/Jupiter, is mind comprehending all there is.) But, once it is accepted that there are connections and patterns and levels of meaning which may not have been apparent to the author, then the author cannot determine how the text is read; and Augustine, who interprets Moses as conveying truths about the Trinity and the Christian Church, is left without defence against the Freudian reading of his own text.

But Augustine, unlike many of his present-day readers, believes that there is a control on multiple readings: there is truth authenticated by the word of God. He has a canon (which is Greek for a rule or standard of measurement) both of text and of interpretation. Scripture is authoritative: you do not select, as the Manichees did, only the bits you like. It is acceptable to find in Scripture a meaning which the writer did not understand, but which was foreseen by the Spirit who inspires the writer with truth; it is not acceptable to find a quite other meaning than the writer intended (*On Christian Teaching* 3.27.38, 1.37.41). There are multiple interpretations of Scripture, but they must be measured against the rule of faith.

This is not a final reply, because of the problem known to theologians as the hermeneutic circle: the rule of faith is itself formulated in accordance with Scripture. Augustine thinks he still has an answer. Suppose he could question Moses himself about Genesis, and get over the initial problem that Moses speaks Hebrew.

How would I know whether he was speaking the truth? If I did know, would it be from him? Within me, within the dwelling-place of my thought, a truth which is neither Hebrew nor Latin nor Greek nor barbarian, without the instruments of mouth and tongue, without the sound of syllables, would say 'He speaks the truth', and I would at once, in full assurance, say confidently to that man of yours, 'You speak the truth.'   (*C*.11.3.5)

Readers have to decide whether they can say the same to Augustine.

12 Narrative and memory

The *Confessions*, then, is a modern book in its awareness of the activity of reading, but not a post-modern book which postulates that there are no correct readings. The Freudian reading is one possible interpretation of a book which can itself be read on many levels, as autobiography, philosophical theology, meta-narrative, cultural transformation – and that is not an exhaustive list. But all readings, however far they depart from Augustine's own interpretation of his life, depend on what Augustine chooses to tell us. The problem of the

Confessions is that of any autobiography: by simplifying the complexities, ignoring the seemingly irrelevant, establishing a structure and a narrative sequence and a style, and above all just by forgetting (*C*.3.12.21), the author edits his or her life. It is literally impossible (not just unreadable) to 'tell it like it is', to record lived experience. Some twentieth-century writers make this point by selecting what is usually rejected, trivial events or chance associations of ideas. Augustine makes it by reflecting on the workings of memory.

When Augustine did memory-training as part of his education in rhetoric, he probably learnt the technique of the *aedes memoriae*, the 'house of memory'. You imagine a regular facade or building and put the items you want to remember in specified places – the successive points of a speech, say, distributed along a row of columns or a sequence of rooms. Then you can mentally scan the facade or walk through the building and find what you have stored. But this, as Augustine says, is a very different matter from remembering the past. Here you are dealing (*C*.10.8.12) with vast rambling houses and tracts of land, something like the ground-plans of late Roman 'great houses' which archaeologists can reconstruct but find hard to interpret. You cannot remember where particular memories are stored, and others thrust themselves on you asking 'Will we do?' Sometimes you have forgotten that there was something to look for. As well as the image of the house – orderly or disorganised – of memory, he has the image of memory as the stomach of the mind (*C*.10.14.21), in which different foods are digested and supply nourishment, but do not retain their distinctive taste.

Augustine is not satisfied with the vague terminology of 'memories': he wants to differentiate memories of events, places, technical terms, emotions. He has to deal with the puzzle that we can remember how we felt without now feeling the same emotion. He revives in book 10 questions he had posed in book 1 about the use of language. In book 1, he cannot of course remember learning to talk, but deduces that he did so by interpreting, and trying to use, body-language and by linking it with the sounds people made in association with particular objects; thus he began to take part in human society (and, in Wittgenstein's terms, to join in language games). Language is stored in his memory, like the objects and concepts associated with language. What he knows, and what he says, depends on memory. But when he talks of God, or the 'blessed life' (the *beata vita*), he cannot say that these are 'in' his memory, or that he knows what he is still struggling to understand. 'Memory' comes to include everything a human mind knows or can know, not just the past experience of a human individual. Once again, what interests him in his own experience is not himself remembering, nor what he can retrieve of his past, but the activity of remembering and what it can tell us about human existence in relation to God. 'This is a force of my mind and belongs to my nature, yet I myself do not grasp all that I am' (*C*.10.8.15): he does not mean that he cannot reach his subconscious memories, but that introspection and reflection on the powers of the human mind is (as the Platonists taught) a route to what transcends the mind.

How do we deal with the jumble of remembered experience? By ordering it into a story, a narrative sequence, which seems to us to make sense, and which in turn calls up other memories or awareness that something has been forgotten. That is what Augustine has been doing in books 1–9, telling as much as he can of how God brought him back to Christian faith. It is worth trying the experiment of asking 'How did I come to be what I am now?', and noticing what you now count as important about yourself, what memories count as explaining it, what might count as a future development of the story. Are you interested in your philosophical position, your human relationships, your social context, the kind of writing you do? Are you telling a Freudian, a Christian, a Marxist, a liberal humanist, or a quite other kind of story?

What interests Augustine in book 10 is the content of the question, the philosophical problems of narrative and time. Narrative is an ordered temporal sequence: this happened, then this, and now ... but what is 'now'? As I sing one of Ambrose's hymns (hymn-singing was an innovation in the west, and Augustine was there when Ambrose introduced it,

C.9.7.15), I move from one sound to the next, remembering what I have just sung and expecting what I shall sing next. I am stretched between what I have done and what I shall do; I measure the long and short syllables, but I cannot measure their duration until they are over, and then they are no longer there to be measured. I cannot explain what I am doing, and what is true of singing a hymn is also true on a larger scale of human life, so that existence in time disintegrates as I try to make sense of it (*C*.11.28.38–29.39). 'You are my eternal father, but I am dispersed in times whose order I do not know, and my thoughts, the inmost entrails of my soul, are torn apart by the storms of change, until I flow together in You, purified and molten by the fire of your love.' The experience of time is *distentio animi*, not just an extension of the spirit over remembered past and expected future, but a distension or pulling apart of the soul.

13 Telling stories

When we think about it, according to Augustine, existence in time disintegrates, and so does the possibility of narrative, and indeed of any communication. Augustine was as aware as any Derridean critic of the factors which actually convey meaning and cause acceptance, and of the gap between words spoken and their reception. (He discusses this in *The Teacher*.) Nevertheless, like many critics who think communication is strictly impossible, he can still order a narrative better than most. He had been trained to select, structure, present, to hold the interest of an audience and to pre-empt, as far as possible, the likely audience reaction. His style proclaims this skill, but he also makes it explicit: he will not allow his readers to cast themselves as passive consumers of rhetoric. On the contrary, he first disconcerts them by talking all the time to God (should they be listening?), then reminds them that they are readers of a text and that they are, as human beings, challenged by what is being read. They are not to lapse into the comfortable satisfaction of curiosity. Book 10 insists that we think about what it might mean to love God and to try to live as God wants. 'People are curious to know about other people's lives and slack about amending their own. Why do they ask me to tell them who I am, when they do not want You to tell them who they are?' (*C*.10.3.3). That is the point of having a human audience for a confession directed to God.

Rhetorical skill – as Augustine also reminds us – is doubly suspect. It is a technique bound up with pagan culture and formed on pagan models, as in his own study of Cicero and Virgil: how can anyone use the technique without creating for himself and his readers an intertext of unholy literature and false ideals? Christians in the late fourth century were beginning to convince themselves that they could use the style but transform the content. But why should they need the techniques of pagan falsehood to make Christian truth convince? We have been warned to stay alert and not to be taken for a ride. Yet it is very hard not to be caught up in Augustine's story and to read it as a true and moving account of one man's conversion; and when it was suggested (Courcelle, *Recherches*) that the story was too good to be true, many readers obviously felt they had lost something which mattered to them greatly.

14 Augustine's conversion

Augustine selects, as an archetypal account of human sin, his theft of fruit (*C*.2.4.9) from a forbidden tree – not because it was good fruit, or because he needed it, but for the satisfaction of breaking the rules; and this episode comes in the context of adolescent lust. The critical break with his past life, the moment at which he resolves to live in chastity, comes in a garden, under a fig-tree. Augustine hears a voice 'like a child's' (*C*.8.12.29) chanting two words of Latin, *tolle lege*, 'pick up and read'. He takes this as a message from God, opens his book – 'the book of the Apostle', which always means Paul – and finds a verse which summons him to chastity.

So Augustine, who has sinned as Adam did by taking forbidden fruit and has become subject to sexual desire, is rescued under the tree from which Adam and Eve took fig-leaves to hide their genitals. The words which tell him what he must do are those of Paul, the archetype of the sinner instantly converted: a 'Damascus road experience', such as happened to Paul, is still a familiar phrase. And Augustine, whose life had been shaped by the written word, acknowledges that he was looking for a text to change his life. Antony's life had been changed by 'go, sell all you have, and give to the poor, and you shall have treasure in heaven', and he had just been reminded of Antony by the story Ponticianus told (*C*.8.6.15) of the secret policemen converted by reading Antony's life. Is it all too carefully shaped to be true? He dramatised the debate between his old loves and the Lady Continence (*C*.8.11.26−7): has he done the same to the rest? Has he made a story into a plot?

It was fifteen years before Augustine wrote the *Confessions*, and the episode in the Milan garden may have taken on new resonances for him as he thought about it: inevitably, he writes in retrospect, looking for the origins of the person he is at the time of writing. A man in his forties, established in a pattern of life, is not likely to see things as he did at thirtysomething, when other options were real possibilities. In 386 Augustine was responding quite differently to the transformation of his life, living in a peaceful house at Cassiciacum with a family group (something you would not guess from the *Confessions* − his mother, his brother, his son and two cousins). They were joined by Alypius and by two students with whom Augustine read Virgil before dinner; he discussed philosophy and recorded his conclusions in tranquil philosophical dialogues. In the *Soliloquies* he wrote at the time, talking not to God but to Reason, he considers his own reactions very much in the tradition of moral self-examination. ('So, you have rejected wealth and power, but are you quite sure you do not want a charming, cultured wife, with just enough money of her own, who would not obstruct your pursuit of philosophy?') The vital text from Paul does not feature in the work of these years; nor, indeed, does Paul feature as the liberated sinner.

This is not to say that nothing happened in a garden at Milan. Some people do have sudden and dramatic experiences of being freed from compulsion, and the *sortes Biblicae*, the practice of opening the Bible (apparently) at random, does usually supply a verse which can be interpreted to fit the situation. People used to do *sortes Virgilianae* too, with equal success; and *sortes Augustinianae* also work, as they did for Petrarch (see chapter 6). (The sample reference in the Preface, *C*.10.18.27, was provided by *sortes*, and an even better one was provided for a helpful philosopher, who, like Augustine, finds Aristotle's *Categories* really quite straightforward. He found *C*.4.16.30: 'I was not aware that these arts are extremely difficult even for hard-working and intelligent people to understand, until I tried to explain them.')

Augustine's 'conversion' was not a sudden event. Intellectually and spiritually he moves through several stages of conversion, inspired by his reading of *Hortensius* and of the 'Platonic books' and by the example of people he admired (*C*.8.5.10). Some time elapses between his moment of liberation and his decision to be baptised and to lead a monastic life. This mixture of imperceptible process and moment of decision is quite believable. It is like C.S. Lewis's realisation, as he sat on the top deck of a bus in Oxford, that his philosophical position did now imply belief in God - a fact which did not, at the time, encourage him at all. Lewis, another man of great literary sensitivity, did not exploit the symbolism of this undramatic moment. (A Pilgrim's Progress in a place of scholarship, but by a conveyance accessible to all?) Nor does Augustine explicitly make the connections pointed out by Courcelle and others; but his training made him just as capable of seeing, or constructing, the pattern. What is theologically vital to Augustine, at the time of writing the *Confessions*, is his liberation from the chains of sin, and specifically from sexual compulsion, by the reading of a biblical text and his God-given response to it. It may be too good a story to be true, but how can we say, against Augustine, that it did not happen? Stories are made by the telling, and what needs telling will change over time. 'Time is not empty and does not roll ineffectively through our senses: it does remarkable things to the mind' (*C*.4.8.13).

Chapter 4

Speaking the truth: rhetoric and style

In recent years it has been the fashion to argue that there is no truth, no final and correct account of anything, but only manners of description which for the moment evoke a response in the audience: rhetoric is all. (Is it then true that there is no truth?) For those who think that there is truth, or at least that some claims can be shown to be false, rhetoric may seem unnecessary or even dangerous. The problem arose for Augustine because Christians were committed to the belief that ordinary people might understand Christian truth more directly and profoundly than the highly educated. The professional speaker loses his authority not because there is no knowledge for him to have, but because there is truth and it is only by God's grace, not by professional skill, that he can help his audience to understand. How, then, should he set about it?

15 *Sermo humilis* and variation of style

Christian preachers in late antiquity sometimes felt bound to reject any conscious use of rhetoric: they preferred *sermo humilis*, 'ordinary speech'. Rhetorical skill aimed to please the highly educated, but their congregations included ordinary working people – and, of course, women, who very rarely had more than primary education. Moreover, the study of rhetoric was (as in Augustine's own education) bound up with the study of pagan authors, and the New Testament seemed to be written in a quite different style. Twentieth-century scholars brought up on 'the classics' find New Testament Greek disconcertingly naive and even incorrect; educated men in the fourth century had much the same reaction to the Greek or Latin Scriptures. It is only in the last few decades that the *koinê* ('common') Greek of the New Testament has been put in the context of professional but non-literary prose. Augustine takes it for granted that Jesus' disciples were uneducated men, speaking the language of fishermen, *sermo piscatorius* (the equivalent, perhaps, of the dockside at Hippo). Even the style of Paul, who is by far the most rhetorical of the New Testament writers, could be a problem. Jerome carefully explains that Paul is not really uneducated, but is writing in Greek, a language which does not come easily to him – he thinks in Hebrew.

But *sermo humilis* is not absence of style. It is one particular style – and it was Cicero who invented the name. *Sermo humilis* is more ordered and coherent than everyday speech; it has a carefully chosen vocabulary and carries a risk of condescension. (Ambrose is a major source of information on ancient wrestling techniques, because he uses wrestling metaphors as present-day clergy use football.) Augustine's experience with the Manichees, he says (*C*.5.6.10), taught him that neither fluency nor simplicity is a guarantee of truth. 'I had learned from You that nothing should seem true just because it is eloquently said, or false just because the lips make sounds which are awkward; and again that a thing is not true because it is said without polish, nor false because the style is splendid.' In his *On Christian Teaching* he argued that rhetoric could legitimately be used in the service of Christian truth. Anyone (he said in the maddening way of the very clever) could pick up the rules of grammar and style, without going through the traditional training. The Bible itself uses the major rhetorical techniques, so they do not necessarily belong to a corrupt pagan culture. Variation of style is quite proper, and does not imply that you think some aspects of Christian truth are more important than others which you expound in a simpler manner. Sometimes you are explaining, sometimes approving or disapproving, sometimes trying to 'bend' your hearers, to make them actually behave differently. The 'ordinary' style is obviously suited to explaining and the exalted style to influencing your hearers. The 'moderate' style, *genus temperatum*, is designed to please, and this is acceptable provided your aim is to help your audience to some good, not to show off your own skill. When Augustine reread the *Confessions*, he noted one passage which seemed to him to fail the test. He had quoted some familiar thoughts on friendship, saying that he and the friend who died at Thagaste were like one soul in two bodies; and he had suggested (*C*.4.6.11) that he was afraid to die himself because then his friend would have died altogether.

In the *Confessions*, Augustine uses all the available 'registers' of style and moves between them with great rapidity, even within a sentence. Some of the most impressive passages depend on very simple vocabulary and syntax arranged with great skill in a setting of much greater elaboration. Here is one famous instance:

sero te amavi, pulchritudo tam antiqua et tam nova, sero te amavi! et ecce intus eras et ego foris, et ibi te quaerebam, et in ista formosa quae fecisti deformis inruebam. mecum eras et tecum non eram. ea me tenebant longe a te, quae si in te non essent, non essent. vocasti et clamasti et rupisti surditatem meam, coruscasti, splenduisti et fugasti caecitatem meam, fragrasti et duxi spiritum et anhelo tibi, gustavi et esurio et sitio, tetigisti me et exarsi in pacem tuam.

(*C*.10.27.38)

Late I loved you, beauty so old and so new, late I loved you! Look, you were within and I was outside and sought you there, and I rushed, unlovely, to those lovely things which you made. You were with me and I was not with you. Those things kept me far from you, which, if they did not exist in you, would not exist. You called and cried out and shattered my deafness, you blazed and shone and drove away my blindness, you were fragrant and I drew breath and pant after you, I tasted and am hungry and thirsty, you touched me and I was on fire for your peace.

Here patterns of repetition, variation (especially in the responses of the 'five spiritual senses') and word-play are combined with shifts of rhythm and vocabulary from the deliberately simple to the consciously grand. Sharp contrast and change seem to have been a fashion in late antiquity, where the visual arts display the same liking for bright and multiple colours, complex and lively patterning (Roberts, *The Jeweled Style*). The display of skill which an audience can appreciate was preferred to the 'art of concealing art'. Augustine uses rhyme and assonance, in particular, far more than his classical models would approve. It drives his translators to despair: what can they do with *o rara caritas, o cara raritas*? But I think it is not just an ornament of speech, but one more device for making the reader take notice. Rhymes and quasi-rhymes and puns have been coming back into literary fashion because they raise readers' awareness of how words work (consider 'textual harassment', a useful phrase for the negative presentation of female characters). Augustine is quite incapable of using a word inattentively: the *Confessions* is the book of a man who listens to what he says and tries to understand what it implies both by logic and by association. He will use any available technique to make his readers equally aware of what he is saying and they are reading.

16 Intertexts: Bible, classical culture and philosophy

All of us bring associations to what we read, and respond more willingly to a book (as to a person) if we have associations in common. This – often undeclared – baggage is the intertext, the reading 'between the lines' which the author cannot control but can try to evoke. In the *Confessions*, Augustine takes it for granted that his readers are people like himself, who can hear what he is saying because the rhythms of Virgil and the Latin Bible are part of their lives (just as Shakespeare and the King James Version were for generations of English readers), and because they are trained to be aware of language and literature. So the intertexts of the *Confessions* are very prominent, and are of great importance in making the link between Augustine and his readers.

The Bible: Latin and Hebrew

Christian preaching style in late antiquity entailed constant reference to the Bible, sometimes in extended quotation, sometimes only by allusion to a familiar phrase or story. The *Confessions*, in places, are almost a cento of biblical texts – literally a 'patchwork', a fabric made by sewing together pieces of material – especially when Augustine is expounding Genesis. But the influence of the Bible extends beyond quotation. The rhythms and idioms of Hebrew prose and poetry, translated into Latin, are essential to Augustine's Latin style in the *Confessions*, just as Milton's English style was affected by the Latin constructions he could use so fluently.

As with New Testament Greek, the effect of 'Christian Latin' is disconcerting to the classically trained reader. The most pervasive difference is a preference for linking clauses with 'and', as in Hebrew narrative, rather than subordinating one to another as in classical Latin. (The technical term is 'parataxis' as opposed to 'hypotaxis'.) This increases the intensity of contrast and movement which is so characteristic of Augustine. Here is an instance (*C*.7.10.16):

et inde admonitus redire ad memet ipsum intravi ad intima mea duce te et potui, quoniam factus es adiutor meus. intravi et vidi ...

And admonished from there [i.e. the Platonist books] to return to myself, I entered my inmost parts led by you, and I was able because you had become my helper. I entered and saw ...

Most of the paragraphs in book 7 begin with 'and'. The subject-matter is the impact on Augustine of the Platonic books which inspired him to seek God by the ascent of reason from lesser things, and the contrast of Platonist and Christian doctrine. This particular sentence, like the chapter it begins, is influenced by Plotinus, but the style imposes the Bible on Plotinus even when Plotinus is not being brought into line by Bible quotation (a tactic which Augustine had first met in Ambrose's sermons at Milan) or, as here, by transformation of what he says. Plotinus did not invoke God as a guide for the journey into himself. In the last chapter of book 7, Augustine's impassioned gratitude to God has overwhelmed his Platonist attempt, and the words of the Bible dominate and dismiss the books of the Platonists (*C*.7.21.27).

In them no one sings, 'Shall not my soul be subject to God? for from him is my salvation; he indeed is my God and my saviour, my supporter; I shall not be moved any more.' No one there hears him calling, 'Come to me, you who labour.' They disdain to learn from him, because 'he is meek and lowly of heart'. 'For you have hidden these things from the wise and prudent and revealed them to the little ones.' And it is one thing to see from a wooded summit the homeland of peace, and not to find the way to it, and try in vain through pathless places while fugitive deserters beset and ambush you with their leader 'the lion and the dragon', and another to keep to the road which leads there, maintained by the care of the heavenly emperor, where those who have deserted the army of heaven do not attack like brigands, for they avoid it like torture.

A second noticeable effect is 'parallelism'. Hebrew poetry, as in the Psalms, very often works by making a point, then restating it in slightly different form. The rhythms are very distinctive, and preserve some of their effect both in Latin and in English translation. Here is an example, from the psalm Augustine most often cites in the *Confessions*. I have used the version of the Book of Common Prayer (1662), because its cadences are both familiar and unfamiliar to (some) present-day English readers, much as those of the Latin Bible were to Augustine's audience.

> Like as the hart desireth the waterbrooks:
> so longeth my soul after thee, O God.
>
> My soul is athirst for God, yea even for the living God:
> when shall I come to appear before the presence of God?
>
> My tears have been my meat day and night;
> while they daily say unto me,
> Where is now thy God?
>
> Now when I think thereupon, I pour out my heart by myself:
> for I went with the multitude,
> and brought them forth into the house of God.
>
> In the voice of praise and thanksgiving
> among such as keep holy-day.
>
> Why art thou so full of heaviness, O my soul,
> and why art thou so disquieted within me?
>
> Put thy trust in God,
> and I will yet give him thanks for the help of his countenance.
> (Psalm 42 verses 1–7; 41 in Greek and Latin versions)

It is often illuminating to set out Augustine's text in the same visual form (this is done to great effect in O'Donnell, *Augustine*). His Latin prose does not, of course, correspond neatly to the Hebrew, but there is a structural resemblance. Here, I think, is a small example: Augustine is baffled by the problem (see 12) of how we can measure time (*C*.11.22.28).

> My soul is on fire to know this thing:
> this most intricate enigma.
>
> Do not shut them off, O Lord my God, kind father;
> by Christ I implore you, do not shut off from my longing
> these familiar and hidden things;
>
> so that it might not enter into them
> nor they be illuminated by the light of your mercy, O Lord.
>
> Whom shall I question about these things?
> And to whom shall I more profitably confess my ignorance?
>
> My zeal is no annoyance to you
> as it blazes in the study of your scriptures.

Hebrew idiom also nurtures Augustine's liking for strongly physical imagery, which may well have been 'dead metaphor' in Hebrew and even in Greek, but is alive to the point of aggressiveness in Latin translation. 'Mind' and 'heart' are especially likely to be affected, because they are the homes of thought and emotion. Thus, finding importunate memories thrusting themselves on the attention, 'with the hand of my heart I drive them away from the face of my memory' (*C*.10.8.12); and earlier Augustine tries (*C*.4.5.10) to 'move the ear of my heart close to your mouth'. (Dorothy Sayers reports a prayer by a well-meaning curate: 'Lord, teach us to take our hearts and look them in the face, however difficult it may be.') 'Memory is the stomach of the mind' (*C*.10.14.21), which seems to be Augustine's own invention, almost draws an apology from him: it is, he says, laughable, but not entirely irrelevant, to compare memories of happy or sad things to sweet or bitter food which remains in the stomach but is no longer tasted.

Classical culture

But the Bible is not the only intertext. Virgil and the classical cultural tradition also evoke the shared memories of Augustine and his educated readers. Virgil's hexameters cannot successfully form part of a prose text, except in direct quotation (as at *C*.8.2.3, where Augustine is relating the conversion of Marius Victorinus, and constructs an immense Ciceronian sentence, heavy with superlatives and subordinate clauses and adorned with a classical tag, to express the status of Victorinus at Rome). But classical prose can. When Augustine wrote the *Confessions*, the prose rhythms of the classical tradition could not be taken for granted: some literary works were already using the new rhythms called the *cursus*, more suited to Latin as it was then spoken. (Augustine remarks in *On Christian Teaching* that Africans had trouble distinguishing the long and short vowels which were the basis of classical metre.) But the *cursus* does not appear in the *Confessions*. As Augustine describes his study of the 'liberal arts', his style becomes smoothly Ciceronian (*C*.4.16.30); and when he tells us how he won a school prize for rhetoric, he moves between the style in which he excelled and a cry of protest against it:

ille dicebat laudabilius, in quo pro dignitate adumbratae personae irae ac doloris similior affectus eminebat, verbis sententias congruenter vestientibus. ut quid mihi illud, o vera vita, deus meus? quid mihi recitanti adclamabatur prae multis coaetaneis et conlectoribus meis?

(C.1.17.27)

That one spoke most admirably, in whom, appropriate to the status of the character, there stood out the more convincing expression of anger and resentment, the words suitably clothing the sentiments. What was this to me, o my true life, my God? Why did my recitation win applause in preference to my many fellow-students and fellow-declaimers?

This clumsy translation aims to bring out Augustine's shift of register. Two very Ciceronian sentences, complex in structure and polysyllabic in vocabulary, describe the contest he won by excelling in Virgilian emotion and Ciceronian dignity. They surround a brief, simple, near-colloquial cry to God. Its opening, *ut quid*, is a piece of Christian Latin (translated from Hebrew) evoking the Bible; its emotional intensity contrasts with the kind Augustine had so successfully represented. The contestants were to express, in prose, the feelings of Virgil's Juno, who attempts to thwart what she knows to be the divine purpose for Aeneas because it threatens her own commitments and disregards her claims for respect as the consort of Jupiter. In the *Aeneid*, Juno (like most of the other female characters) is the voice of desire thrust aside: Virgil gives great eloquence to those whose claims he denies, just as Augustine speaks in the voice of the culture he rejects to others who will respond to it.

Philosophy

One other voice is often heard: that of the philosophy which Augustine also at last rejected. Plotinus, so Porphyry tells us, would not give set lectures to expound his philosophical system. He preferred discussion with his students, sometimes circulating the results in the form of short treatises, which Porphyry collected and organised in the *Enneads*. Plotinus offers questions, provisional solutions, objections, revised solutions which raise still further questions, far more than exposition – though he could also write brilliant inspirational passages. We do not have enough material to say for certain whether Plotinus' style, even in Latin translation, was as distinctive as (for instance) Wittgenstein's – but it seems a good guess that Augustine fell for it. He would have been very happy in Plotinus' seminar, over a century earlier, raising questions which were given all the time they needed. Of course there are differences, as there are (see 9) between Augustine and the tradition of moral philosophy. He is aware of dealing with questions which may be beyond human understanding or may be obscured by his sin, and he appeals for God's help in dealing with them; he lacks the confidence of Plotinus and Porphyry in the attainments of God-given reason. (Plotinus was made really angry by the claim of the Gnostics that some people had privileged access to a truth which could not be reached by reason.) But Augustine tackles philosophical questions in the same style. Here, for instance, is Plotinus reflecting on the theory that the soul may retain memories of previous existence (*Ennead* 4.3.28):

We had better ask first which power of the soul it is that remembering accompanies. Is it that by which we perceive and by which we learn? Or does remembering desirable things also accompany the power by which we desire, and remembering things which make us angry accompany the assertive power? Yes, someone will say: there will not be one thing which enjoys, and a different thing which remembers what the first thing enjoys. If that is so, the desiring power is moved by what it has enjoyed when it sees the desired object again – obviously by memory, because, if not, why should it not be moved when it sees something else, or sees it differently?

And here is Augustine, also reflecting on memory, asking how it is that he can seek for the happy life, the *beata vita* (*C*.10.20.29):

I do not have it until I say 'Enough: that's it.' So I ought to say how I seek it: by remembering, as if I had forgotten it but still recall that I have forgotten, or by an urge to learn the unknown, whether that is something I have never known or something I have forgotten so completely that I do not ever remember I have forgotten. Surely the happy life is that which everyone wants, and there is no one who really does not want it? How did they know it to want it like that? Where did they see it to love it? We do have it, I do not know how. There is another sense in which a man is happy at the time when he has it, and there are people who are happy in hope. These people have it in a lesser form than those who already are happy in the thing itself, but they are nevertheless better than those who are happy neither in the thing nor in hope. But even they, unless they had it in some way, would not want so much to be happy: and it is most certain that they do want that.

17 Hearing the *Confessions*

Very few twentieth-century readers bring anything like these intertexts to the *Confessions*, and these comparisons can only go some way to explain why Augustine writes as he does. There are, inevitably, other differences in our response to the text. The modern reader faces a printed page. A Latin text will probably note at the foot of the page any 'variant readings', different words offered in different manuscript copies of the text, from which the editor has chosen in accordance with his or her opinion about the reliability of a particular copyist, or about the way errors usually arise in manuscript traditions, or about Augustine's style. (This is what a classicist means by textual criticism.) So the modern reader knows, for instance, that there is a choice to be made in the account of Augustine's conversion (*C*.8.12.29). A voice 'like that of a boy or girl' called 'take and read, take and read'. Was it in the *neighbouring* house, *in vicina domo*, or in the *divine* house, *in divina domo*? If it was the neighbouring house, this was another instance of an apparently chance happening − a child at play − which Augustine interpreted as fulfilling God's purpose. If it was a voice from heaven, the problem of 'what really happened' (see 14) becomes more complex.

Fourth-century readers of Augustine could not make this choice. They had acquired a copy, made by hand, probably by asking a friend (as Alypius asked Paulinus for a copy of Eusebius' *Chronicle*). They may well not have been readers, but listeners to someone reading the text, as in the discussions of Augustine and his friends; the experience of reading and hearing 'in time' and in sequence (see 12) must have been very vivid for them. Even if they were reading to themselves, they are likely to have 'heard' the written words, just as Augustine did whether he dictated or wrote them. The *Confessions*, he says, are uttered silently to God and aloud to people (*C*.10.2.2). It is, in fact, very likely that they were spoken aloud − that is, that he dictated them. He was trained to speak fluently, remembering and improvising at need, and dictation would go some way to explain his amazing output of work and, more important, his extraordinary intensity of style. He could talk to himself, to God and to his imagined audience, with a shorthand writer in the corner, instead of drafting and re-drafting and checking back − we do not know how much revision he did. So Augustine, and Augustine's audience, heard the words of the *Confessions*. But what about present-day readers? Most people now hear the words and rhythms when silently reading poetry, but present-day readers respond to the *Confessions* as prose.

It is possible, and often illuminating, to set out the text as in printed texts of the Psalms (see 16). But the usual effect is prose − quite straightforward prose, in many versions, when the translator has decided that it is most important for the reader to grasp what is being said, and chooses the 'register' of ordinary professional language, the *sermo humilis*, more often than Augustine does. It is really very difficult, in the twentieth century, to find a grand style which does not provoke incredulity; life was easier in that respect for the seventeenth-century translators who found the rhythms of the King James Version quite natural. But that is not the only difference. Modern texts do not only have word-divisions and punctuation, but are divided into helpful paragraphs and chapters (this was an innovation of the early printed versions, from which two different systems survive to give the two sets of numbers). And when Augustine, without warning, moves from his own words to those of Virgil or the Bible, modern texts italicise, or add quotation marks, and give references. All these visual cues were lacking for readers of the first manuscript copies. (The earliest surviving manuscript, the 'Sessorianus', may have been written in the late fifth century, not very long after Augustine's death.) The audience Augustine expected had to 'hear' changes in his writing.

It is often deduced, from Augustine's awed description (*C*.6.3.3) of Ambrose silently reading, that in late antiquity people habitually read aloud. When this question surfaces in scholarly debate, it is always settled in favour of silent reading unless there was an audience (or what would life have been like in the great libraries?). On the level of ordinary human contact, Augustine had hoped that Ambrose would draw him into discussion – and Ambrose was probably hoping he and his friends would go away. On another level of interpretation, it must be important that Ambrose reads but does not speak. Plato said that books are a bad way of doing philosophy, because you cannot argue with a book. Augustine, after long experience of teaching, thought that what one person says has no traceable connection with the flash of understanding in another person. Books spoke to him more persuasively than people (as in the case of Faustus the Manichee). Ambrose, the man who had no time to talk, made it possible by his preaching for the Bible to speak to Augustine. (Ambrose once told

Simplicianus that Paul is not really difficult: you just have to read him aloud.) When Augustine finally ventured to write to Ambrose, he asked which books of the Bible – 'which of Your books', he says to God – he should read. Ambrose recommended Isaiah. Augustine tried, but put it aside until he had more practice in understanding the Lord's style (*C*.9.5.13).

Chapter 5

Finding meanings: Augustine at Carthage

The different 'voices' in Augustine's style can be heard in other authors; but though Virgil and Cicero and Plotinus and the Latin Bible spoke to others besides him, no one else achieved a personal tone in which all of them could be heard. Because the *Confessions* is so 'polyphonic', it is particularly difficult to extract a passage for more detailed examination, and once the choice is made it is difficult to stop quoting and to resist making more and more cross-connections. In the Introduction, I suggested two literary models (from Virgil and the Psalms) for Augustine's experience as he began his further education at Carthage, aged seventeen. Here, to illustrate some of the themes of this discussion, is what he wrote about it himself, perhaps twenty-five years later.

veni Carthaginem et circumstrepebat me undique sartago flagitiosorum amorum. nondum amabam et amare amabam et secretiore indigentia oderam me minus indigentem. quaerebam quid amare, amans amare, et oderam securitatem et viam sine muscipulis, quoniam famis mihi erat intus ab interiore cibo, te ipso, deus meus, et ea fame non esuriebam, sed eram sine desiderio alimentorum incorruptibilium, non quia plenus eis eram, sed quo inanior, fastidiosior. et ideo non valebat anima mea et ulcerosa proiciebat se foras, miserabiliter scalpi avida contactu sensibilium. sed si non haberent animam, non utique amarentur. amare et amari dulce mihi erat magis, si et amantis corpore fruerer. venam igitur amicitiae coinquinabam sordibus concupiscentiae candoremque eius obnubilabam de tartaro libidinis, et tamen foedus atque inhonestus, elegans et urbanus esse gestiebam abundanti vanitate. rui etiam in amorem, quo cupiebam capi. deus meus, misericordia mea, quanto felle mihi suavitatem illam et quam bonus aspersisti, quia et amatus sum et perveni ad vinculam fruendi et conligabar laetus aerumnosis nexibus, ut caederer virgis ferreis ardentibus zeli et suspicionum et timorum et irarum atque rixarum.

rapiebant me spectacula theatrica plena imaginibus miseriarum mearum et fomitibus ignis mei. quid est, quod ibi homo vult dolere luctuosa et tragica, quae tamen pati ipse nollet? et tamen pati vult ex eis dolorem spectator et dolor ipse est voluptas eius. quid est nisi miserabilis insania? nam eo magis eis movetur quisque, quo minus a talis affectibus sanus est, quamquam, cum ipse patitur, miseria, cum aliis compatitur, misericordia dici solet. sed qualis tamen misericordia in rebus fictis et scenicis? non enim ad subveniendum provocatur auditor, sed tantum ad dolendum invitatur et auctori earum imaginum amplius favet, cum amplius dolet. et si calamitates illae hominum vel antiquae vel falsae sic agantur, ut qui spectat non doleat, abscedit inde fastidiens et reprehendens; si autem doleat, manet intentus et gaudens.

lacrimae ergo amantur et dolores. certe omnis homo gaudere vult. an cum miserum esse neminem libeat, libet tamen esse misericordem, quod quia non sine dolore est, hac una causa amantur dolores? et hoc de illa vena amicitiae est. sed quo vadit? quo fluit? ut quid decurrit in torrentem picis bullientis, aestus immanes taetrarum libidinum, in quos ipsa mutatur et vertitur per nutum proprium de caelesti serenitate detorta atque deiecta? repudietur ergo misericordia? nequaquam. ergo amentur dolores aliquando. sed cave immunditiam, anima mea, sub tutore deo meo, deo patrum nostrorum et laudabili et superelato in omnia saecula, cave immunditiam. (*C.*3.1.1–2.3)

I came to Carthage, and there seethed about me on all sides a cauldron of criminal loves. I did not yet love, and I loved to love, and with a more hidden need I hated myself for needing less. I looked for an object of love, loving to love, and I hated tranquillity and a road without snares, because there was hunger in me from the inner food, you, my God, and I was not famished with that hunger, but I was without longing for incorruptible foods, not because I was full of them, but the more famished, the more disgusted. And so my soul was not in good health, and, covered in sores, flung itself outside, wretchedly eager to be scratched by contact with things which can be felt. But if they had no soul, they would not be loved. Love and being loved was sweeter to me if I enjoyed the body of a lover. So I polluted the spring of friendship with the squalor of desire, and overcast its clarity with hellish lust, and though repellent and ugly, I was eager to be stylish and civilised, in my overflowing vanity. I leapt into love, by which I wanted to be caught. My God, my compassion, with how much gall, and with what kindness, you seasoned that sweetness, because I was loved, and I attained the bondage of enjoyment, and was happy to be fastened in the chains of misery, so as to be flogged with the red-hot irons of jealousy and suspicion and fear and anger and quarrels.

I was carried away by stage plays full of images of my misery and fuel for my fire. Why is it that in that place a person wants to feel pain for grievous and tragic happenings which he does not want to experience himself? Yet he wants to experience pain from them as a spectator, and the pain itself is his pleasure. What is this but wretched insanity? A man is the more moved by these things, the less he is in health and untouched by such experiences; yet, when he suffers them himself, it is called misery, and when he suffers with others, compassion. But what sort of compassion, for fictitious events on stage? The man who hears is not being called on to help, but is only invited to feel pain, and the more he feels pain, the more he approves of the author of these images. And if these ancient, or fictitious, human disasters are enacted in such a way that the one who watches does not feel pain, he goes off in disgust, complaining; but if he does feel pain, he stays, intent and happy.

So tears and pain are loved. Yet everyone wants to be happy. Is it that, since no one likes to be miserable but everyone likes to be compassionate, because compassion cannot occur without pain, for this one reason pain is loved? This too comes from that spring of friendship. But where is it going? Where does it flow? Why does it run down into that torrent of boiling pitch, the monstrous surges of foul lusts, into which it is transformed by its own inclination, diverted and degraded from its celestial calm? Then is compassion to be rejected? By no means. So let pain sometimes be loved. But beware of impurity, my soul, under your guardian, my God, the God of our fathers, praiseworthy and exalted in all ages, beware of impurity!

This translation is as close as possible to the Latin text, so that those who know little or no Latin may still be able to see something of how Augustine's language works. But I cannot translate some of the ways in which his language creates associations. In the first sentence there is a word-play on *Carthago* (Carthage) and *sartago* (cauldron) — the 't' and 'th' sounds would not have been distinct — to establish the theme of emotional turmoil: no one has yet found an English equivalent. (In *C*.6.7.11 Carthage is a whirlpool seething with frothy shows, and sucks in Alypius.) The second sentence presents a different problem. Because Latin is an inflected language, words can be grouped for maximum impact, and a few words can be made to carry a heavy charge of meaning without the risk that compression will entirely lose the sense. Augustine likes to do this from time to time, but it is not always clear what exactly he means. The sentence says, very literally, 'I did not yet love and I loved to love and with a more hidden need I hated myself needing less.' Augustine has just mentioned criminal loves, so we might reasonably think he is talking about love-affairs, and means that he was not yet in love with any one person, but was in love with the idea of being in love and disliked himself for not feeling that need more strongly. But what is the 'more hidden need'? Is it the same as the unrecognised hunger for 'inner food' which he goes on to mention? If so, he might mean that he hated himself for not yet being in love, although in this respect he was less needy than in his lack of conscious longing for God. In his *On the Happy Life* (written at Cassiciacum before his baptism) he said that unhappiness correlates with the neediness, *egestas*, of the soul, which in turn correlates with the soul's inclination towards things that change and perish.

Translators have to manoeuvre between 'love' and 'in love', but Augustine does not make this distinction. He interprets his life as a belated recognition that his love is for God: *sero te amavi*, 'late I loved you' (*C*.10.27.38). The passage we are considering now is illuminated by another passage in *Confessions* 10:

per continentiam quippe colligimur et redigimur in unum, a quo in multa defluximus. minus enim te amat qui tecum aliquid amat, quod non propter te amat. o amor, qui semper ardes et numquam extingueris, caritas, deus meus, accende me!   (*C*.10.29.40)

By continence [literally 'holding together', *continentia*] we are brought together and reintegrated into unity, from which we have dispersed [literally 'flowed away', *defluximus*] into multiplicity. A man loves you less if he loves something together with you which he does not love for your sake. O love [*amor*] which always burns and is never extinguished, charity [*caritas*], my God, set me on fire!   (*C*.10.29.40)

Here the stream which flows away from its source, distraction by lesser loves, and love as a fire reappear with a more explicit theological context. The Platonist concern for unity as against multiplicity, for focus on God not on the diversity and mutability of human existence, combines with Augustine's central theological concern. All human love, in Augustine's theology, is liable to be corrupted by the desire to possess, *concupiscentia*. Concupiscence entered human existence when Adam and Eve attempted to take control of their own lives and turned away from God: human society was corrupted, and relations of dominance and possession replaced natural hierarchy and co-operation. To be 'in love' is to be in the grip of desire. Even friendship, *amicitia*, a form of love which should be free from desire, can be a distraction from the love of God if we try to make it our only support (*C*.4.8.13). English cannot supply a range of words which makes explicit the link between *amor* and *amicitia*.

Love is evoked only by sentient, potentially responsive, beings, a point which Augustine (characteristically) makes immediately after he has compared his desire for sensory contact to a man scratching his sores – with dirty fingernails, he adds a little later. This is, at least, a kind of loving: if these physical things had no soul, they would not be objects of love. Even the 'love of pain and tears' can be justified in so far as pain and tears are necessary to compassion, and compassion is a manifestation of love. This is not as uncontroversial as it may sound. Stoic philosophy argued that, although the good man will act to relieve suffering because he is aware of 'belonging' to all the world, he will not 'suffer with' (the basic meaning of 'compassion'). To do so would be no help, and would allow his soul to be churned up and confused by vicarious distress. (Relief workers often come to the same conclusion about the proper response to disaster.)

The manifestations of love are balanced by the manifestations of misery. Again, there is a problem for the translator in preserving the associations of words. *miseria* means a state deserving pity, but *miserabilis* (pitiable) can no longer be translated by English 'miserable', as in the often misunderstood phrase 'miserable sinners', and 'pitiful' (like 'wretched') has acquired an overtone 'contemptible'; whereas *misericordia* (a heart full of pity) has to be rendered as 'mercy' or 'compassion'. So another set of Augustine's word-echoes cannot be heard, and we lose one of his ways of telling us that real compassion takes no pleasure in what is really pitiable – namely, turning away from God. The point is made very clearly in book 1:

quid enim miserius misero non miserante se ipsum et flente Didonis mortem, quae fiebat amando Aenean, non flente autem mortem suam, quae fiebat non amando te, deus, lumen cordis mei et panis

oris intus animae meae et virtus maritans mentem meam et sinus
cogitationis meae?   (*C*.1.13.21)

What is more pitiable than a pitiable man who does not pity himself
and weeps for the death of Dido, which came about by loving Aeneas,
but does not weep for his own death, which came about by not loving
you, God, light of my heart and bread of the mouth within my soul
and strength which is husband to my mind and recesses of my thought?

This spectacular sentence uses several of Augustine's favourite rhetorical devices: accumulation of related words (*miserius
misero non miserante*), balanced structure (*flente ... quae
fiebat amando ... non flente ... quae fiebat non amando*),
and a range of biblical and often strongly physical metaphor.
The message is developed in book 3, as God's *misericordia*
is contrasted with the spurious compassion of the theatre-goer
or lover of literature, who 'suffers with' only in a very limited
sense: no real suffering is happening to anyone and only an
emotional response is required.

Here, the translator is baffled by two Latin verbs with double
meanings: *dolere* means both 'to grieve' and 'to feel physical
pain' (yet 'distress' sounds too weak); *pati* means both 'to suffer'
and, more mildly, 'to undergo' or 'to experience'. The Greek
word *pathos* means something that happens to you, like a nasty
experience or (in our terms) an emotion. Augustine is working
here in the philosophical tradition which assumes that emotions
do not come out of you: they come from outside and attack you,
like germs, and if you are in good spiritual health you do not
succumb. He uses just this metaphor in remarking that a man
who is free from emotional disease, *sanus a talibus affectibus*, is
not easily moved by the theatre. Philosophical thinking on the
emotions was already being modified by the experience of
Christian ascetics in their solitary struggle, and the biblical
language they used to describe it: sometimes they had to with-
stand the attacks of the devil, but often it was the promptings
of their own heart. But, on the assumption that an emotional
state is something you undergo, Augustine can play on the para-
doxes of fake suffering (because nothing awful is really happening), genuine suffering (because pain is really felt) and enjoyable
suffering — the last a well-known philosophical problem.

In book 4, these questions recur as Augustine remembers real grief for the death of his friend.

> I was wretched, and wretched is every soul fettered by the love of mortal things, and it is torn apart when it loses them, and it feels the wretchedness which makes it wretched both then and before it loses them. Thus I was in that time, and I wept most bitterly and took my rest in bitterness. I was wretched, and felt my own life of wretchedness to be dearer than my friend.   (*C*.4.6.11)

Conscious misery is a kind of relief, almost enjoyable in real distress. Unreal events, presented by a skilful dramatist and actors, evoke a kind of real suffering in the spectator, who is generalised from Augustine's own experience, very much in the tradition of moral self-analysis. Meanwhile, the real suffering of Augustine's soul, voluntarily trapped in the snare of physical love, is hidden from him by the literary imagery of the suffering lover, which is probably what he saw on stage; we do not know exactly, but he mentions elsewhere stage versions of Virgil, and explicit dramatisations of the love of Attis for the goddess Cybele.

Augustine uses every cliché in the tradition to describe his state: chains, fire, anguish, the lover lashed by jealousy. It was possible, under the laws of the late Roman empire, for a man in chains to be tortured with red-hot iron, though usually it was metal plates, not the rods which Augustine has combined with fire and iron in a near-absurd image of love's victim. So Augustine in love is a first spectacle of possible, but fake suffering which causes real, but welcome, pain; and he can move from it to his speculations on why people enjoy tragedies. The narrative of his life halts, as so often, while he reflects on the much more important question of the extraordinary way people behave. The vocabulary and the register shift from the consciously dramatic ('I rushed headlong into love ... the theatre snatched me away') into the neatly analytic, with simple vocabulary and balanced phrase; and then the clear stream of reflection is once again made turbid by metaphor and anguished appeals to God.

Augustine's metaphor of the stream which becomes a swirling torrent is as much a literary cliché as the tormented

lover – perhaps it was more vivid for readers who regularly saw
Mediterranean watercourses turn into rivers in spate. It is also
taken to extremes – the torrents of boiling pitch belong in
Hades, just as, in the first appearance of the metaphor, the
'hellish lust' is literally the Tartarus of lust, the deepest and
darkest place in some imaginings of the pagan afterworld, where
the wicked are punished. But this time he wants to convey a real
and destructive experience, not a false image derived from
literature. Perhaps he is working with images appropriate to his
state of mind at the time; he did not, on rereading the *Confessions*, label this passage as 'frivolous declamation' or
showing-off.

The stream first appears in the extraordinary pile-up of
metaphors which present Augustine's state of mind and soul. He
hated tranquillity (*securitas* is literally the absence of cares) and
a 'road without snares': this is one of the disconcerting moments
when he switches into biblical idiom (from Wisdom 14.11).
muscipuli are mousetraps, and whereas 'snares' is a dead
metaphor (with Latin equivalents), 'mousetraps' is not. He was
hungry, but misinterpreted his hunger: it was 'from' –
presumably 'caused by the lack of' – inner food, namely God.
This is a familiar Christian metaphor, contrasting physical with
spiritual food, and Augustine extends it with a medical obser-
vation, that people lose their appetite when they have not eaten
what they need. Malnutrition causes poor health, especially
sores (a condition Augustine must often have seen), and his
ulcerated soul flings itself on the outside world to relieve the
itching by physical contact. Any Christian reader would think of
Job, the archetype of misery, when Satan afflicted him with
boils: he sat in the ashes and scraped himself with a potsherd
(Job 2.7–8). A reader with a philosophical background would
also have in mind Plato's argument that physical pleasure is only
the scratching of an itch – no itch, no pleasure. This point links
up with the experience of the theatre-goer: no pain, no pleasure.

At least, Augustine says, the objects of love are sentient
beings. But he wanted bodily enjoyment, not just emotional
response; so he polluted the spring of 'friendship', of non-
possessive love (cf. *C.*5.16.26). Its contamination is expressed

in heavy words and insistent alliteration, *coinquinabam sordibus concupiscentiae candoremque eius obnubilabam de tartaro libidinis*, which are suddenly lightened by a mention of the civilised young man, *elegans atque urbanus*, or so he thought in his 'emptiness'. Then one of Augustine's brief, pointed sentences ('I rushed into love, longing to be caught') makes the transition to more metaphor and more anguish: gall in sweetness and the torments of the lover.

The contaminated stream soon reappears, diverted and polluted 'by its own inclination': this is not a natural progress from human concern to love, nor an external force misdirecting the flow of affection, but a corrupt choice of possessive desire. Augustine exhorts his soul and invokes his God, both (at first sight) in somewhat conventional style. The heavy repetition of *cave immunditiam*, 'beware impurity', is interrupted by an appeal to God the soul's guardian; for readers who knew their Bible, there was a further message here. The words invoking God are those which begin the prayer of the 'Three Holy Children' who praised God in the burning fiery furnace (Daniel 3.52 in the Vulgate; the continuation, still in regular liturgical use, is the 'Benedicite'). The fires of lust will eventually be transformed by the blazing love of God which fuses the disintegrated soul (*C*.11.29.39), and the stream which flows away from its source into pollution and turmoil will be brought back to purity. To use Augustine's preferred image, his restlessness will end in Sabbath rest, as he brings his own work to a close with a meditation on God's good works. 'There are some good works of ours, by your gift, but not everlasting; after them we hope to be at rest in your great sanctification; but you, who are the good, lacking no good are always at rest, because you are your own rest' (*C*.13.38.53).

Chapter 6

Reading the *Confessions*

Augustine, and any other classically trained orator, would recognise this chapter as what modern scholars call a *recusatio*, that is a refusal which is also an explanation why one cannot do the task assigned − in this instance, to trace the influence of the *Confessions* in literary tradition.

The problem of 'influence'

The *Confessions* is, in some obvious ways, one of the most influential books of western European culture. It has never dropped out of sight, but has been endlessly reused, reinterpreted and simply recopied. To follow its history would require a large-scale co-operative research project. Courcelle (*Confessions*) produced a monumental volume on the *Confessions* in literary tradition, but, as he acknowledges, this means predominantly French literary tradition, and he could not have done it without the help of several colleagues working in later periods. He found total disagreement on whether Augustine had either followed or established a genre.

Did the *Confessions* establish a genre? In style, they popularised an interweaving of biblical quotation which is in fact quite common in fourth-century Christian literature, and continued to be so in devotional writing and spiritual biography. Innumerable Christian writers have taken from Augustine what they want, or what they recognise. Christian religious have used the *Confessions* for exactly the effect that Augustine noted, to arouse the human mind and emotions towards God. They have found an idiom for prayer, interpreted their own relationship to God in the light of Augustine's, and used him to support their theology. Augustine's style also interweaves philosophy and classical culture: many people, like him, think (and therefore pray) partly in fragments of literature, and he offers them the model of a style in which to do it, and a sense that there are others like them. Classical literature after Homer had always made use of quotation, allusion, reminiscence and reworking: Augustine uses these techniques to convey the self and the thought of a person formed by literature.

In the history of human self-awareness (which Hegel thought was the only history that mattered) the *Confessions* stands out for the acknowledgement of motivations, both conscious and (at the time) below the conscious level, and of the power of words to determine experience. Augustine did not invent either autobiography or the use of one person's life to exemplify the human condition, but he transformed the kind of self-description which could be thought or written. Here was a man of very great intelligence and good (though not the best) education, who, instead of identifying with his reason and belittling lesser concerns, presented himself as full of conflict and uncertainty, convinced of his unworthiness and his dependence on God. This is a new and powerful voice; but the voice is Augustine's, and no one who was not Augustine could write the same kind of book.

Names come easily to mind if one starts to think of writers who must surely have been influenced by the *Confessions*. Boethius, in the *Consolation of Philosophy*, is addressed by a personified Philosophy who owes something to Augustine's personified Continence (*C*.8.11.27). Dante, in the *Divine Comedy*, takes Virgil as his guide (who cannot guide him all the way) in a mid-life journey, an exemplary story of escape from the wilderness of sin, descent into hell and rescue by divine grace. Montaigne tells us 'I am the subject of my book.' Pascal underwent conversions to philosophy and faith. Newman expounds a spiritual journey to his true church. But it is not so easy to explore further from such starting-points.

First, it is not just this one work of Augustine which makes an impact, however much some writers loved it. Boethius, for instance, owes more to the personified Reason of Augustine's *Soliloquies*, the book he wrote soon after his conversion in which, as in Boethius' *Consolation*, God does not speak;

and Montaigne, who greatly admires the *City of God*, does not mention the *Confessions*. It is often Augustine's theology, or (too often) the Augustinianism which hardened into doctrine from his theological experiments and explorations, that can be seen at work, rather than the *Confessions* themselves. Luther, for instance, was a monk in an Augustinian order, and his copy of the *Confessions* has survived, with some frustratingly sparse annotations. What interests him is Augustine's theology of the grace of God, and he cites the *Confessions* in his own theological work chiefly for Augustine's reading of Romans in *Confessions* 8, and for the long-delayed but overwhelming response to Monica's prayers for her son.

Second, great writers may be indebted to, or may in some respects resemble, other great writers, but even when they acknowledge a debt they do not proceed by imitation: it needs another book to consider the interrelations. For instance, Dante in his *Convivio* took Augustine as an example of why one might talk about oneself: 'in the progress of his life, which was from not good to good, from good to better, from better to best, he could give examples and teaching which could not have been received from other truthful testimony'. Images and ideas from the *Confessions* appear in the *Divine Comedy*, but Dante's range of intertexts is as great as Augustine's own, and often he is reading Augustine from the perspective of mediaeval commentators.

There is also negative influence. Opponents of Christianity, or of Augustinian theology, can use the *Confessions* as evidence: this process began in Augustine's lifetime. The British theologian Pelagius, hearing Book 10 read in Rome soon after Augustine had written it, was shocked by the implications of Augustine's prayer 'You command continence: give what you command, and command what you will' (*C*.10.29.40). Did Augustine seriously think that God lays on us commands which we are quite incapable of obeying? There was an obvious counter: did Pelagius seriously think that we can go it alone, relying on good moral training and using prayer and the Bible as an occasional stimulant? The 'Pelagian heresy', often said to be characteristically British, is one example of a permanent theological problem: a partial truth hardens into a position. Time changed Augustine from a controversial theologian to an authority, and his writings acquired canonical status. Interpretations he had offered were taken out of their context in the world he knew and in his own development, and were made into theological principles which it was dangerous to challenge. So attacks on 'the church' can become attacks on Augustine, and the *Confessions* can be used to show him up: in the fifth century it was his having a concubine, in the twentieth it is his sending her away.

The rest of this chapter offers a range of responses to Augustine, to illustrate (very briefly) some of these general points. First, the earliest known examples of books which imitate or respond to the *Confessions* in a cultural context shared with Augustine. Second, two people who used the *Confessions* to intepret their lives to themselves: Petrarch, who was helped to reconcile classical 'humanist' culture with Christian commitment, and Teresa of Avila, who was assured that God could forgive her sins. Third, Rousseau, who used the *Confessions* as a book to react against in rejecting an Augustinian interpretation of human life; and finally, Proust, who is closest to Augustine in his preoccupation with memory, cultural models for experience, and the reinterpretation of the past, but furthest away in his central concerns.

Early imitations

Soon after copies of the *Confessions* were in circulation, at least three other people wrote accounts of themselves which appear to be influenced by Augustine's. Paulinus of Pella wrote an autobiography in Latin hexameters, calling it *Eucharisticus*, 'Thanksgiving': his aim, he said in the preface, was not to record a distinguished career, but to acknowledge the manifestation of God's mercy in his life. Here is the simultaneous rejection and transformation of classical culture which is to be found in Augustine. (Paulinus had a problem with Latin, rather than Greek, because even though he grew up in Bordeaux the family servants were Greek-speaking.)

Paulinus' grandfather Ausonius had been both a poet and a statesman. Ausonius was a friend of Paulinus of Nola, and was both hurt and puzzled by his decision to abandon public life and responsibility for his estates; they exchanged poems on this subject, though not the heavy hexameters chosen by Paulinus of Pella. Hexameters do not lend themselves to philosophical self-questioning or to biblical quotation, so the *Eucharisticus* relates to the *Confessions* in its theme, its choice of episodes, and the occasional turn of phrase.

The *Confessions* of St Patrick of Ireland, despite their title, are even less like Augustine's, to the point that scholars disagree on whether there is any relationship. The general resemblance, again, is in the emphasis on God's mercy for a sinful man, but the opening sentence has nothing in common with Augustine's meditation on invoking God. 'I Patrick, most boorish of sinners and least of the faithful and most despicable among most men, had as father Calpurnius ...' Patrick's prose style includes biblical quotation and reminiscence, but is very much less complex than Augustine's. Here is Patrick's account of the vision which called him to Ireland:

And there I saw in a night vision a man coming, as if from Ireland, whose name was Victoricus, with innumerable letters, and he gave me one of them. And I read the beginning of the letter, which said 'The voice of the Irish', and as I was reading out the beginning of the letter, I thought at that moment that I heard the voice of those who live by the forest of Voclutus which is near the western sea, and they cried out thus as if with one mouth, 'We ask you, lad, to come and walk here among us', and I had great compunction in my heart, and I could read no more, and that is what I experienced.

Ennodius, bishop of Pavia in the late fifth century, was much more like Augustine than Patrick was, for he could happily manipulate Ciceronian style and high cultural references. It is an odd experience to find that so intense a book as the *Confessions*, hardly a century after it was written, has joined the repertory of educated allusion. A friend wrote to Ennodius, who had seen a letter not intended for him, cheerfully comparing this with Augustine's theft of pears and exhorting him to weep

for his faults; Ennodius replied in kind, arguing that Augustine
– unlike him – had stolen something worthless, and quoting
a line from Terence which Augustine quotes in the *Confessions*
(*C.*1.16.26). When Ennodius wrote a brief autobiography
as a thanksgiving for his deliverance from illness, Augustine
provided him with a model for acknowledging the mercy
of God and for repenting his desire for poetic fame: but
his *Eucharisticus* reads very much like the work of someone
who has found a new literary model to try and a new kind
of fame to pursue.

My God, my redemption! What things come to mind of all you
have done with me, and of all that I have done against me! If they
were brought together, no time would be empty of your help or
of my fault. I choose to sample one of your innumerable gifts
bestowed on me, and by passing over myriads to touch upon one
alone of your benefactions. At the time when the longed-for entry
of King Theoderic revived Italy ...

Petrarch: humanism and the Bible

Petrarch, who had many friends in the Augustinian order,
was given a pocket copy of the *Confessions*, in about 1333,
by a particularly learned friend (Denis of Bourg St Sépulcre,
who was both a religious solitary and a Doctor of the University
of Paris). It was immensely important to him: he carried
it with him and his works, especially his letters, are full of
allusions and quotations. The revival of Greek and Latin
culture in his time made Petrarch experience, as Augustine
had, a conflict between the culture which appeared as the
triumph of human reason and the rival claims of Christian
tradition. The *Confessions* made him believe that they could
be reconciled: he observed that Plato and Cicero had helped
Augustine to Christ, and that some of what they said about
God and the soul, contempt for this world and longing for
another, could just as well have been written by Ambrose
or Augustine. The *Confessions* also persuaded Petrarch to
modify his opinion of the Bible as Augustine had done.

There is another work of Augustine, called *Confessions*, divided into thirteen books. In the first nine of these he confesses all the errors and faults of his whole life, from earliest infancy and his mother's milk; in the tenth, the surviving remnants of sin and his present state of life; in the last three his uncertainties about Scripture and often his ignorance. By this *Confession*, if I am any judge, he shows himself to be almost the most learned man ever. If you are led into the habit of reading this book with concentration and devotion, I hope you will never lack pious and salutary tears, tears of shame. I speak from experience. So that you may come more vigorously to this reading by the influence of him you love, know that this book was my way into all the holy scriptures, which, as being lowly and unkempt and unequal to secular literature, in excessive love of the latter and contempt for the former, by a false opinion of myself and — to make a brief confession on my own account of this sin too — by youthful arrogance and, as I now understand and clearly see, by prompting of the devil, for too long, as a conceited youth, I fled. 'This book changed me' (*C*.3.4.7) to the point that — I do not say I abandoned my early sins; if only I had abandoned them at my present age! — but from it I came not to despise or detest holy scripture; on the contrary, little by little scripture calmed that revulsion and drew to itself my unwilling ears and reluctant eyes; and finally I began to love those scriptures, to admire and investigate them, and to pluck from them perhaps fewer flowers, but certainly more fruit than I did from those writings once so beloved. It would have been disgraceful for a Christian to have been wholly unchanged by the eloquence of Augustine, when, as he says in book 3, Cicero's *Hortensius* had changed him so much. If you cannot find these *Confessions* elsewhere, I will send you a copy.

(Letters in Old Age 8.6)

In Petrarch's dialogue the *Secretum*, Augustine is his interlocutor in a conversation witnessed by Truth, challenging him to abandon the ties of earthly love and worldly fame. His conflicts are expressed in a very Augustinian letter to his friend Denis (*Letters to Friends* 4.1) — so Augustinian, in fact, that many people have doubted whether the episode he described can really have taken place. It is, like Augustine's account of his conversion, almost too good a story to be true. Petrarch and his brother climbed, with great difficulty, to the summit of Mont Ventoux near Valchiusa. He began to reflect on the ten years since he had left university at Bologna, and on his own conflicts and frustrations. 'What I used to love,

I do not now love; I lie − I do love, but too little; no, I have
lied again: I love, but with too much shame and sadness; at
last I have told the truth. That is how it is: I love, but something
that I would love not to love, that I would want to hate; I love,
but unwilling, forced, sad, grieving.' It occurred to him to
look at his copy of the *Confessions*: and, like Augustine in
the garden, he found a text. 'People go and admire the heights
of mountains and the vast waves of the sea and great waterfalls
and the circuit of Ocean and the orbits of the stars, but they
leave out themselves' (*C*.10.8.15).

Teresa of Avila: the spiritual life

Teresa, like Augustine, is a Doctor of the Church − with the
considerable difference that she was only acknowledged as
such in 1970, not from her own lifetime in the sixteenth
century. She is also a very different kind of Doctor. As she
acknowledged at the beginning of her autobiography, she
could not write a formal literary style: what she writes is not
an elegantly simple *sermo humilis*, but loosely constructed,
colloquial, and sometimes quite difficult to interpret. Only her
exclamations of praise to God remind the reader of Augustine's
style. She had no formal training in theology or philosophy,
and does not reflect as Augustine does on the implications of
what she says. Yet her *Life* is in many ways very close to the
Confessions, and she says that the *Confessions* changed her life.

Teresa wrote the first version of her autobiography, in
1562, at the request of her confessor, who thought it would be
helpful to him, and to her fellow-nuns, to have an account of
the special favours God had given her in response to prayer.
It was intended for private and very limited circulation to
those who might benefit from it. Inevitably, it was read by
others, and was caught up in controversies about the reform of
religious orders and the dangers of 'interior' prayer. Teresa
modified and added to her *Life* in response to comments from
other religious whom she respected. In its present form, it has
nine chapters of autobiography, in which she narrates her life
with more detail than Augustine, but in a very similar tone.

She praises her parents but comments on the defects of her upbringing (it must be very difficult to bring up a saint); she grieves over wickedness which the less saintly reader – like her own confessor – finds hard to detect. She suggests, but so cryptically that it is difficult to be sure, that she experienced strong sexual desires, and she reports the devastating illness from which she suffered. (Her nausea and paralysis must have been partly psychosomatic: in later life, when she had to travel and negotiate to set up a reformed Carmelite order, she had much better health.) We also learn that she and her favourite brother, as children, used to read the lives of the saints, and decided to win martyrdom by going to convert the Moors; frustrated in this, they took to playing hermits in the orchard, except that the hermitages would keep falling down.

The tenth chapter introduces a much longer account: the next thirty chapters deal with her experience of mental prayer and the trials and favours given her by God. As in the *Confessions*, this tenth section is transitional; the ninth chapter deals with the turning point in her life, sometimes called her second conversion, when she was given a copy of the *Confessions*. If this was the Spanish translation which was dedicated to a friend of hers in 1554, she was perhaps in her early forties at the time of this episode, and had been a nun for twenty years.

'So my soul went on weary, and although it wanted to rest, the wretched habits that it had would not allow it to.' Her way of prayer was changed by an image of Christ wounded. Then

in that time I was given the *Confessions* of St Augustine, which it seems the Lord ordained, because I did not get them and had never seen them. I am very devoted to St Augustine, because the convent where I lived as a secular [i.e. before she became a nun] was of his Order, and also for having been a sinner, because I found great comfort in the saints whom the Lord had turned to Himself after they had been so. I thought there was help to be had from them, and, because the Lord had pardoned them, He might do it for me; except that one thing discouraged me, as I have said: that the Lord had called to them only once, and they had not gone back to falling, and I had done it so often that it distressed me. But thinking of the love which held me, I would return to confidence, because I never lost faith in His mercy; I often did in myself.

Oh, God help me, how the hardness of my soul amazes me, after so much help from God! It frightens me to think how little I could do for myself, and how tied down I was so as not to resolve to give myself wholly to God. When I began to read the *Confessions*, I seemed to see myself there, and I began to commend myself often to that glorious saint. When I reached his conversion and read how he heard a voice in the garden, it seemed just as if the Lord said it to me, as my heart felt. I was for a long time all dissolved in tears, and was in great affliction and distress. Oh, how a soul suffers, God help me, from losing the freedom it had to be its own master, and what torments it endures! It amazes me now that I could live in such torment; praised be God who gave me life to come out of such fatal death!

Rousseau and the rejection of Augustine

Rousseau called his own autobiography *Confessions* in deliberate reference to Augustine. Describing himself in a letter to the Archbishop of Paris, who had condemned his book *Emile*, he quoted Augustine on the need to tell the truth. But what he takes from Augustine is a belief about human nature which he wants to reject. He begins his own *Confessions* not with a meditation on God but with a declaration about himself.

I want to show my fellow-men a man in all the truth of his nature, and that man will be myself. Me alone. I am not made like any of those I have seen; I venture to believe that I am not made like any of those who exist. If I am not worth more, at least I am other. Whether nature did well or badly to break the mould in which she cast me, no one can judge until after reading me. Let the Last Trump sound when it will, I shall come with this book in my hand to present myself before the sovereign judge. I shall say distinctly: this is what I did, what I thought, what I was. I have said good and bad with the same frankness. I have kept silent about nothing and added nothing good ... I have shown myself as I was, contemptible and vile when I was so; good, noble, sublime when I was so. I have unveiled my inner self as you have seen it yourself. Eternal being, gather round me the innumerable crowd of my fellow-men: let them hear my *Confessions*, let them groan over my unworthy acts and blush for my sufferings. Let each in his turn reveal his heart before your throne with the same sincerity, and let a single one say, if he dares: I was better than that man.

(*Confessions* I, Gagnebin and Raymond 5)

Augustine would never have declared himself good, noble, sublime: instead, he would have sighed over past times when he had thought such things. But Rousseau has other standards of human conduct, and he does not confess to God, but to other human beings. He offers several motives for these *Confessions*: to relieve his mind, to give readers some knowledge of a human being other than themselves, to refute accusations, to enjoy his memories of himself. But his purpose is to challenge the way his readers think about human life.

Like Augustine, Rousseau sees childhood as a critical time of life. He denies Augustine's version of the 'cradle argument' in which babies demonstrate the greed, and the desire to dominate, which since the Fall has been innate in the human race. Rousseau believes in original goodness, not original sin: human beings naturally want to survive and prosper, but they have no wish to harm others and do not want to see others suffer. According to Rousseau, children go wrong not because of inherited sin, but because their innate good feelings are corrupted by social hypocrisy and convention. They could, in theory, be reared without corruption, though Rousseau entirely failed to try it out: readers have been horrified by his acknowledgement that he handed his own children over to foundling hospitals.

Augustine stole pears which he neither needed nor wanted, and thinks this shows the human tendency to sin for the sheer satisfaction of breaking the rules and going with the crowd. Rousseau stole apples because he was hungry and because he had started stealing to oblige a fellow-apprentice.

That is how I learned to covet in silence, to hide myself, to dissimulate, to lie, finally to steal — an idea which had not come to me until then, and from which I have never since been able to cure myself entirely. Desire and powerlessness always lead to that. That is why all lackeys are rogues, and why all apprentices should be; but in tranquil and just conditions, when everything they see is within their reach, most apprentices lose this shameful tendency as they grow up. Not having had the same advantages, I could not derive the same profit from them. It is almost always good feelings badly directed which make children take the first steps towards evil. Despite constant privation and temptation, I had stayed over a year with my master without being

able to bring myself to take anything, even things to eat. My first
theft was a matter of being obliging, but it opened the door to others
which had not such a laudable purpose.

(*Confessions* I, Gagnebin and Raymond 32)

Proust: memory and literature

The immediate resemblance between Augustine's concerns and
A la recherche du temps perdu is strong enough to make one
wonder whether Proust had in fact read the *Confessions*,
perhaps while he was at the Lycée Condorcet, where he was
(like Augustine) educated in literature and philosophy. He too
is concerned with the activity of memory, especially with
involuntary memory, with changing perceptions over time,
and with the use of literature to interpret experience, especially
the experience of love. (He differs from Augustine in acknowledging the influence of music and painting as well as literature:
Swann's passion for Odette is strengthened because a pose of
her head and neck reminds him of women in the paintings of
Botticelli.) Here is Proust in *Le temps retrouvé* realising,
comparatively late in life, what the direction of his life has been:

Then a new light occurred in me, less dazzling, to be sure, than that
which had shown me that a work of art was the only way to rediscover
lost Time. And I understood that all these materials for a work of
literature were my past life; I understood that they had come to me,
in frivolous pleasures, in laziness, in affection, in suffering, stored up
by me without my guessing at their destination, their very survival,
any more than the seed putting in reserve all the foodstuffs which will
nourish the plant. Like the seed, I could die when the plant had
developed, and I found that I had lived for it without knowing,
without its seeming to me that my life ought ever to come in contact
with those books I should have liked to write, and for which, when
I used to sit down at my table, I could find no subject. So all my
life up to this day could, and could not, be summed up under the
heading: A Vocation. It could not, in the sense that literature had
played no part in my life. It could, in that this life, the memories of
its sadnesses, of its joys, formed a reserve like the albumen in the
ovule of plants, from which the ovule draws its nourishment to
transform itself into a seed, at the time when it is still unknown
that the embryo of a plant is developing, but the embryo is nevertheless
the site of chemical and respiratory phenomena, secret but very

active. Thus my life was in touch with that which would bring about its maturation.
(Clarac and Ferré 262)

In *A la recherche du temps perdu* Proust, like Augustine, narrates, then halts the narrative while he reflects on its implications for his primary concerns. But his narrative presents the detail of social relationships, and his primary concerns, though some of them have the same names as Augustine's, are entirely different. 'Love' means human love, the 'time' that is lost is past human experience; the human past, including the past self (or selves) of a human being, is destroyed by the passage of time but can be saved by literature, specifically by the creation of new metaphors that make a fresh connection between sensation and memory. Memory, in Proust, works quite differently from memory in Augustine. In his early work *Jean Santeuil* he has the image of the past as an archive of photographs, which may fall open at some forgotten episode. (The comparison was not, of course, open to Augustine, but it is odd that Augustine never thinks of painting as a kind of memory.) For Augustine memories are jumbled up, half-forgotten, nourished by reading and experience which has been digested and has lost its specific flavour: involuntary memory may come, but not invoked in its totality by a repeated experience like Proust's eating his madeleine.

Above all, the purpose is different. Like Augustine, Proust thinks we must go into ourselves to find the real world, but that means our memories of time past, not the ascent of reason towards God. Proust's father was a practising Catholic, but God is nowhere in Proust's work, and if he quotes the Bible, it is as a literary allusion. He does, later in *Le temps retrouvé*, move from the image of the 'seed which dies' to its biblical archetype.

I said to myself not only 'Is there still time?' but 'Am I in any state to do it?' The illness which had done me a service in making me − like a harsh director of conscience − die to the world ('for if the grain of wheat does not die after it is sown, it will be alone, but if it die, it will bear much fruit'), the illness which, after laziness had protected me from facility, would perhaps guard me from laziness, the illness had used up my strength and, as I had long since noticed, especially at the moment when I stopped loving Albertine, the strength of my memory. Now the recreation by memory of impressions which must then be deepened, illuminated, transformed into equivalent understanding, was not that one of the conditions, almost the very essence of the work of art as I had conceived it just now in the library?

(Clarac and Ferré 437.)

Proust does not rely on any strength but his own; immortality, for himself and his remembered past, can only come from literature.

Conclusion: the 'Confessions' now

In a century which seems to be rejecting both the classical canon which formed Augustine and the Christian doctrine he helped to form, the *Confessions* still find an audience, not only among Christians. In T.S. Eliot's *The Waste Land* Augustine is one of the fragments shored against the ruin of European culture, and the *Confessions* is briefly set alongside the Buddha's Fire Sermon as a voice of western asceticism. It seems extraordinarily little to take from so intelligent a text as the *Confessions*, but perhaps that is the point. In fact, far more has survived the ruins.

Theologians and philosophers continue to debate Augustine's theology and his arguments on time, memory and language. Wittgenstein (himself much given to confession) took from the *Confessions* a theory of language − not, in fact, Augustine's theory − which he challenged in the *Philosophical Investigations*, arguing for 'language games' which we learn by playing them, as against words with a clear relation to things. The concerns of literary critics are moving closer to those of traditional philosophy, as they reflect not only on the techniques of constructing a work of literature, but on the power of words and patterns of thought to interpret or even construct human experience. They are interested in Augustine's awareness of the activities of writing and reading (thus Paul Ricoeur's influential *Time and Narrative* starts from *Confessions* 11) and on the relation of language, and literature, to reality. They approve of Augustine's refusal to assert authorial control over his own life and his own writing, even when they do not share his belief that there is an authority which we can partially understand. If Augustine had said, in Derrida's notorious phrase, 'there is nothing outside the text', he would have meant 'there is nothing that is not expressed in the Scripture which God gave us'; but he is most willing to acknowledge the multiplicity and endlessness of human interpretation.

The questions which interest social historians, historians of ideas and educated readers generally, are very much what they were in the fifth century. The cultural transformations of 'late antiquity', which the *Confessions* document, raise problems which we still face. What makes a brilliant product of the educational system throw up his worldly career and his sexual satisfaction? What beliefs are implied about human nature, the existence of God and God's relationship to people, the interpretation of human frustration and conflict? Did Augustine make the right choice, or was he, like the others he inspired, a victim of his own rhetoric?

Augustine wanted readers to use his book to look at themselves, and that is what they have done, though not always in the sense he meant it: some have looked at themselves in the sight of God, others have looked at their own image. I shall end by taking something (*C*.6.11.18) for myself and others in a profession which Augustine once followed.

I shall set my feet on the step where my parents placed me as a child, until the plain truth is discovered. But where is it to be found? When is it to be found? Ambrose has no time; there is no time for reading. Where do I look for the books? Where or when do I buy them? Who would lend them? There must be set times and hours assigned for the health of the soul ... My students occupy the morning hours: what do I do with the rest? Why not this? But when do I visit the important people whose support I need? When do I prepare material for the students to buy? When do I restore myself by relaxing my mind from its preoccupations?

Guide to further reading

The periodical *Revue des Etudes Augustiniennes* includes an annual update of work on Augustine: this runs to sixty or so pages, several of which are always on the *Confessions*. I have deliberately kept these suggestions for further reading very brief. All items listed, except the older translations, have extensive bibliographies of their own.

Texts

The Latin text generally used by present-day scholars is the critical edition by M. Skutella (Leipzig 1934), which was printed with notes and a French translation by A. Solignac in the *Bibliothèque Augustinienne*, vols. 13–14 (Paris 1962), and has been revised by H. Juergens and W. Schaub (Stuttgart 1981) and by L. Verheijen in the series *Corpus Christianorum* (Turnhout 1981). The new critical edition by James O'Donnell, with a detailed commentary, 3 vols. (Oxford 1992), was published after the final version of this Landmark was submitted, so (much to my regret) I was unable to use it.

Translations

Two translations of the *Confessions* are most likely to help the present-day reader by their liveliness and clarity. These are the Penguin Classic by R. S. Pine-Coffin (Harmondsworth 1961) and the outstanding version by Henry Chadwick (Oxford 1991).

Earlier translations have an interest and charm of their own, especially those based on the seventeenth-century versions in which the rhythms of the King James Version are very close to the rhythms of ordinary prose. The pioneering work of Sir Tobie Matthew (1624) was revised by William Watts (1631) and many times since; E. B. Pusey's version (1838, once described as 'incense-wreathed') is in effect a new translation; a further revision of Watts appears in the Loeb Classical Library (London 1912) with a facing Latin text (that of P. Knöll 1909). Many readers still use F. J. Sheed's translation (London and New York 1943). But these earlier versions have been overtaken by recent work on the text, and on the intellectual context, of the *Confessions*.

Social and intellectual context

Three British scholars have made an exceptional contribution to the
understanding of Augustine's world: Peter Brown, Henry Chadwick
and Robert Markus. I single out three of their many writings.

Peter Brown, *Augustine of Hippo: a Biography* (London 1967) has
been described as 'biography without the theology', but remains aware
of theological questions and evokes the settings of Augustine's life with
Augustinian intensity. The book also includes useful chronological
tables of Augustine's work and lists of translations.

Henry Chadwick, *Augustine*, in the Past Masters series (Oxford
1986), is deliberately concise and focusses especially on the philosophical context, which is also supplied in the introduction and
annotations to his translation.

Robert Markus, *The End of Ancient Christianity* (Cambridge 1990),
is a most perceptive survey of the transformations of thought which
took place in Augustine's lifetime and the century that followed.

James O'Donnell, *Augustine* (Boston 1984), is another brief introduction which has a particular sympathy with Augustine's literary and
theological purposes.

Three older works are still very helpful. F. van der Meer, *Augustine the
Bishop* (English translation London and New York 1961, reprinted
1983), affectionately and vividly presents Augustine's pastoral work as
priest and bishop of Hippo. John Burnaby, *Amor Dei* (London 1938,
reissued 1991), and Gerald Bonner, *St Augustine of Hippo: Life and
Controversies* (London 1963, new edition 1986), cover intellectual
biography and theological debate.

Brent Shaw, 'The family in late antiquity: the experience of
Augustine', *Past and Present* 115 (1987) 3–51 quarries the *Confessions*
for information on family life.

All recent work on the *Confessions* is indebted to Pierre Courcelle,
Recherches sur les Confessions de Saint Augustin (Paris 1950, revised
1968): for those who read French, this is an impressively documented
but lucidly written book.

Language and style

There is a vivid response to 'Christian Latin' and its ethical implications
in Erich Auerbach, *Literary Language and its Public in Late Latin
Antiquity and in the Middle Ages* (London 1965). Several recent books
are helpful on the cultural context:
Robert Lamberton, *Homer the Theologian* (Berkeley, Calif. 1986),
explains the techniques of exegesis which Christian writers share with
non-Christian.

Robert Kaster, *Guardians of Language: the Grammarian and Society in Late Antiquity* (Berkeley, Calif. 1988) deals with the methods of literary analysis, and the use of literature as an index of culture, which Augustine would have learned and taught.

Michael Roberts, *The Jeweled Style: Poetry and Poetics in Late Antiquity* (Ithaca and London 1990), discusses Christian and non-Christian literary preferences.

Averil Cameron, *Christianity and the Rhetoric of Empire* (Berkeley, Calif. 1991) is concerned with the transformation of discourse (that is, ways of speaking and describing) and discusses Augustine on rhetoric.

On Augustine and Virgil, see Camille Bennett, 'The conversion of Vergil: the *Aeneid* in Augustine's *Confessions*', *Revue des Etudes Augustiniennes* 34 (1988) 47–69.

Danuta Schanzer, 'Latent narrative patterns, allegorical choices and literary unity in Augustine's *Confessions*', *Vigiliae Christianae* 46 (1992) 40–56, is perceptive on Augustine's reworking of literary models.

On 'Nachleben', Pierre Courcelle, *Les Confessions de Saint Augustin dans la tradition littéraire* (Paris 1963) is thoroughly documented but, like so much writing on 'influences', not very illuminating on the ways in which Augustine inspired later authors. Some good examples of a sensitive approach to 'influences' are Anna Crabbe, 'Literary design in the *De consolatione philosophiae*', in *Boethius: his Life, Thought and Influence* ed. Margaret Gibson (Oxford 1981); Ann Hartle, *The Modern Self in Rousseau's Confessions: a Reply to St Augustine* (Notre Dame 1983) and John Freccero, *Dante: the Poetics of Conversion* (Cambridge, Mass. 1986). The texts from which Rousseau and Proust are cited in chapter 6 are: J.-J. Rousseau, *Œuvres Complètes I: Les Confessions et autres textes autobiographiques*, ed. B. Gagnebin and M. Raymond (Bibliothèque de la Pléiade, 1959); and Marcel Proust, *Le temps retrouvé*, text established by P. Clarac and A. Ferré (Gallimard 1954).

Biography and character

Two papers by Christopher Gill and Christopher Pelling in Christopher Pelling (ed.) *Characterisation and Individuality in Greek Literature* (Oxford 1990) are only marginally concerned with Augustine, but clear on questions of character and development in biography.

Patricia Cox, *Biography in Late Antiquity* (Berkeley, Calif. 1983), is more difficult reading: she also does not discuss Augustine, but is concerned with the presentation of the 'holy man'.

Paula Fredriksen, 'Paul and Augustine: conversion narratives, orthodox traditions and the retrospective self', *Journal of Theological Studies* ns 37 (1986) 3–34, is particularly helpful on Augustine's changing perspective.

Twentieth-century psychological approaches to Augustine are presented in a collection of papers from the Society for the Scientific Study of Religion: *The Hunger of the Heart: Reflections on the Confessions of Augustine*, ed. Donald Capps and James E. Dittes (1990).

Philosophy

The philosophical context is discussed in detail in the *Cambridge History of Later Greek and Early Mediaeval Philosophy* (Cambridge 1970), edited by A. H. Armstrong, with outstanding chapters by Armstrong himself on Plotinus and by Robert Markus on Marius Victorinus and Augustine. Readers who are inspired by this to try Plotinus will find the translation by A. H. Armstrong in the Loeb Classical Library (7 vols., London 1966–88) more lucid than the triumph of style in Stephen MacKenna's version (London 1917–30, revised edition 1956), but the recent abridgement of MacKenna by John Dillon in Penguin Classics, *Plotinus: the Enneads* (Harmondsworth 1991) has very useful editorial material.

Christopher Kirwan, *Augustine* (London 1989) continues to engage with Augustine's arguments on language, evil, creation and time.